UNLEASH
YOUR FULL
POTENTIAL
AND LIVE YOUR ULTIMATE LIFE

**Awaken the infinite power within and
create the life of your dreams**

D1246676

Warren Veenman & Sally Eichhorst

Reach Publishers
Kwa-Zulu Natal, South Africa

By Warren Veenman & Sally Eichhorst
Dare To Succeed
Where Has My Ceiling Gone?
A Pocket Full Of Inspiration

By Sally Eichhorst
If I Can You Can

Copyright © 1998 Warren Veenman & Sally Eichhorst

All rights reserved. No part of this publication may be reproduced, stored in a retrieval system, or transmitted in any form or by any means, electronic, mechanical, photocopying, recording, or otherwise, be lent, resold, hired-out, or otherwise circulated without express written consent of the authors.

ISBN 0 620 22865 2

Printed and bound by Pinetown Printers (PTY) LTD, Pinetown
Edited by Janine Williams and Sian Chaplin
Cover picture supplied by Great Stock

Contents

Introduction   5

Part 1 Time, Friend or Foe
Chapter   1   Time is of the essence   11
Chapter   2   Wasting our precious time   17

Part 2 Unleash the Infinite Power Within You
Chapter   3   The power of thought   27
Chapter   4   The spreading poison of negative influences   31
Chapter   5   The hidden world of the subconscious   35
Chapter   6   You are what you think   39
Chapter   7   The secret to controlling your thoughts   43

Part 3 Conquer the Mental Obstacles that Limit You!
Chapter   8   Stop worrying!   51
Chapter   9   Fear!   57
Chapter   10   Can you beat depression?   69
Chapter   11   Avoiding depression!   73
Chapter   12   How to drive out negative mental states   79
Chapter   13   Secret to happiness   91

Part 4 The Road to Attaining Your Dreams
Chapter   14   Why goals?   99
Chapter   15   What do you really want?   103
Chapter   16   Create a burning desire to reach your dreams   107
Chapter   17   The plan   111
Chapter   18   Believe in yourself   117
Chapter   19   Utilise the techniques of affirmations and visualisation   123
Chapter   20   Perseverance   133
Chapter   21   Dreams can come true   139

Part 5 Use your mind and body to overcome all
Chapter   22   Got a problem?   143
Chapter   23   The powerful influence of physiology   151

In conclusion   155

Introduction

'A journey of a thousand miles must begin with a single step.'
Lao-tzu, 'Tao Te Ching'

People from all walks of life have applied the basic principles outlined in the following pages and have succeeded beyond their wildest expectations, just as you can. They have earned more money, found more happiness and in general lived fuller lives.

This book will open the door to your mind and the tremendous potential that lurks therein. It will help steer you in the right direction by limiting those mental obstacles such as fear, worry, depression and failure which hold so many of us back from achieving success. It will also show you a step-by-step plan to achieve anything you've only ever imagined.

This book will also inspire and point, if not lead you in the direction of success. It will help you change your life for the better by reminding you that you alone hold the key that unlocks the potential power within yourself. It will show you the road to tapping into your inner strength, so that you can plan the life and enjoy the success you have always only imagined.

This is not your average run of the mill, 'read me once and file me away to be forgotten' kind of book. On the contrary, this book is designed to be kept indefinitely and to be reviewed whenever you feel the need for direction and motivation in your life.

So whatever your dreams and aspirations may be, whether you desire more money, power, fame, love, happiness or anything that success encompasses for you, we believe that by following the principles outlined in this book, you can achieve and live your dreams.

Have you noticed that those who succeed in life are not necessarily the best looking, the strongest, the most educated or the most intelligent among us? They also may not enjoy the luxury of a supportive family, financial security or similar advantages to help them succeed. Indeed, many of whom success is expected, fail and conversely, many who seem doomed to failure, succeed.

Success has nothing to do with your physical status, background, financial security or education. One need only look at someone like the late Franklin Delano Roosevelt who in spite of spending most of his life in a wheelchair after an attack of polio, was the only American President to serve four terms of office. Charlie Chaplin, the famous comic actor came from a poor and underprivileged background. His father was a drunk and his mother was often out of work, yet he became the most famous and talked about comedian of his time. Wilma Rudolph was born to a poor family and was struck by double pneumonia and scarlet fever, leaving her without the use of her left leg, requiring her to use special shoes to enable her to walk again. Despite all this, she became a remarkable athlete, winning 3 gold medals in the 1960 Olympic Games.

The point is, we all have one thing in common; the potential to achieve our dreams and attain happiness in life, no matter what our circumstances may be. You too have the potential to achieve virtually anything you want. You were born with unquestionable capabilities and already possess what it takes to achieve literally whatever you desire.

So if we all have the power within us to achieve anything we want, then why do so many people never achieve their dreams and feel permanently unfulfilled? **The solutions lie within the pages of this book!**

Whilst reading this book, we strongly recommend that you do the following:

★ Read each chapter carefully, highlighting sections that make an impact on you.

★ Once you have completed the book, go back and review these highlighted sections.

★ Once read, this book should be kept close at hand and referred to often, to keep you motivated and moving in the right direction.

★ Don't rush through these pages. Think about what you are reading and apply what you learn along the way. Only then will this book be of benefit to you.

Part1 – Part 3 of this book aims to open the door to your mind and unleash its full potential. This will mentally prepare you for Part 4, which will show you, step-by-step the road to living your ultimate life.

It is a statistical fact that up to ninety percent of people who read a book do not finish it. Even more shocking is that they do not reach the second chapter. Is it any wonder that many of these people don't succeed in life? They lack the drive and effort so necessary for them to reach their dreams.

We urge you not to fall into this percentage and rather to read on and enjoy the ride with us. It's a journey that will change your life.

You are now ready to embark on your journey......

Part 1

Time
Friend or Foe

CHERISH THE MOMENT

A second, a minute, an hour, a day, a year; yet another swept away before my eyes.
I watch in desperation, knowingly letting them slip by, yet yearning to stop them at all costs.
Every precious and lost moment feeding upon my conscience.
Why did I not try harder to make them last instead of wishing them away doing unliked tasks.
Most of us spend our lives doing monotonous, routine jobs, merely so we can survive this money hungry jungle.
We long for weekends and holidays, writing off the rest.
Is it not pitiful that we do not cherish every precious second that is ours.
How dare we wish away this gift of life, more precious than anything man can own.
Live for today and don't count on tomorrows.
Tomorrows build up, becoming lost, empty castles of yesterdays; leaving barren, forgotten lands of time gone by.
Cherish each moment for it may be your last!

Sally Eichhorst

Chapter 1

Time is of the Essence

'We haven't the time to take our time.'
Eugene Ionesco, 'Exit the King'

Is it not shocking how we abuse our valuable, priceless and limited store of time here on earth? We should be spending it wisely, investing it carefully and enjoying it wholeheartedly. Instead, think about how often we have been guilty of wasting this precious resource. How many times can you recollect uttering the following phrases?

'I need to kill some time.'
'Let's blow some time at the mall.'
'Time is passing me by.'
'I'm really pressed for time.'
'It was a waste of time.'
'Time means nothing to me.'
The list goes on!

Why do we waste so much of our precious time? Why do some procrastinate, leaving things for another day, while others live in the past, neglecting the present?

Could it be that so many of us live under the misconception that we have all the time in world? Possibly we haven't given much thought to the importance of time. Maybe we feel we'll always be around, untouched by the passage of time. It seems that many of us may suffer from a misguided and totally unrealistic feeling of immortality. We seem to have forgotten that we all have a time limit on our lives and whether we like it or not, accept it or not, our time here on earth will eventually run out.

What we should be doing is cherishing each and every day. But what do most of us do? We wish our days away, living only for weekends and holidays.

We simply cannot afford to 'wish our days away' as life is far too short. It is amazing how many people are ignorant regarding this fact. They believe that they have an outrageously exaggerated number of days available to them, when in fact they don't.

How do we know this?

We have asked numerous people from all walks of life this simple question: **'What do you believe the average life-span in days is for a human being?'**

It is no wonder that people believe they have all the time in the world, considering their answer to the above question is so astoundingly off track! Most of the answers range from one hundred thousand right up to a million days. Can you believe these figures? Think about it. If you were born a hundred thousand days ago, you would be over 270 years old. Now if you were born a million days ago, you would be over 2 730 years old. (You'll certainly make The Guinness Book of Records!)

When we explain to people that the average life-span of a human being is only 27 375 days (75 years), they often don't believe us until they work it out for themselves.

Take a few seconds now to let this figure sink in. Become aware of just how precious each and every one of your days is.

You only have an average of 27 375 days to live from birth. If you are thirty years old you have already spent nearly 11 000 of your precious days. This means that you have less than 16 500 days left. So don't waste your time and wish even one of these priceless and invaluable days away. Life is simply too short to waste!

Yet, of the millions of people all over the world who die every day, most have wasted their lives. They never really enjoyed the ride. They never took the risks that offered bountiful rewards, never stood up for themselves and their beliefs, never loved for fear of losing it, never reached for their dreams or set goals for fear of criticism or failure, never accomplished much due to procrastination and sheer laziness.

Unknowingly, they wasted their lives! If these people could have their lives over again, do you think they would now cherish and make the most of every precious second? You bet they would!

'I wasted time, and now doth time waste me.'
Shakespeare, 'Richard II'

Every second counts!

At the start of every new-born day, you are handed 86 400 seconds with which to do as you please. No matter who you are, whether you are a famous celebrity, the richest man in the world or a worker in the fields, you are given an equal amount of seconds each day. No one gets one second more!

These precious seconds tick by so quickly and disappear forever. We have to make each second count so that it benefits us in the future. In other words, we must make the best of each moment and situation, every day of our lives. There is only one way that your seconds will ever be of benefit to you and that is to profit in the future from time spent today. What do we mean? For starters, you could study further in your field. You could read books that will enhance you mentally. You could work on improving your physical condition. In fact, there are countless ways to make the most of your seconds.

Einstein, Henry Ford, Christopher Columbus, Isaac Newton, the Wright brothers - they all had 86 400 seconds a day. They made the most of it. So can you!

Think about this. If you awoke to a new day and were told that this was your last, how would you spend each second of it and how different would it be from your time spent the previous day?

You will probably find that your behaviour, actions, frame of mind, attitude and overall outlook would be totally different. You would certainly want to make the most of every second!

In essence we should live every day as though it were our last, for we have no way of knowing if indeed it may be. Surely none of us wants to leave this world wishing for so much more from life. Make it happen now!

> *'Lost yesterday, somewhere between sunrise and sunset,*
> *Two golden hours, each set with sixty diamond minutes.*
> *No reward is offered, for they are gone forever.'*
> **Horace Mann, 'Aphorism'**

Living in the past

James (not his real name) was a temporary security guard at a building we frequented. He loved to chat and would always try and corner us for a bit of chit-chat on our way in or out.

James was your typical 'past orientated' person. Whenever he spoke to us, he would always speak about his wonderful past. This one sided conversation always consisted of the same stories, repeated over and over. He complained endlessly, comparing everything to the good old days, when everything was so much easier, safer and cheaper. Without fail the conversation would then steer towards his sporting achievements at school and the award he received over 5 years ago for best security guard at his previous job. Never once did we hear James talk about his plans for the future. It was as though his life was over already and all he had was the past.

James is like so many people out there. His thoughts are dominated by his past. He has no burning desire for a better future, no major goals in life, no drive to better himself and grow as a person. He is just existing from day to day with no direction in life. As long as he has enough money for food and clothing he is satisfied.

A few months ago we happened to bump into James who was working in a temporary position at a hardware store. We had not seen him in over 5 years. We spoke to him for a few minutes and in that time he again complained about how he missed the good old days. He told us once more about his achievements at school and the award he once won for best security guard.

This is a prime example of a man squandering his precious time by living in the dead and distant past.

You cannot live in your past and expect your future to take care of itself. To succeed in life you must live for today and invest in tomorrow.

There are millions upon millions of people who, like James, prefer to live their lives in times dead and gone. They dwell on what they had or could have had.

To move forward and progress in life they have to let go of the past. It's impossible to make something worthwhile of their future if they're living in the past. Why waste your time thinking about what you had or could have had when there is nothing you can do about it? That time is gone. Forget the past, especially the old wounds, which you unnecessarily carry with you through life. Remember, when you dwell on past hurts and injuries today, you open up fresh wounds for tomorrow. So leave your past behind you and embrace your future.

This is worth repeating and should be imprinted forever on your mind:

" When you dwell on past hurts and injuries today, you open up fresh wounds for tomorrow!"

When your thoughts are always on past victories, previous relationships, opportunities missed and mistakes made, you create within yourself feelings of insecurity, worry, fear and uncertainty which adversely affects your future decisions.

Don't misunderstand us, it's normal and good to keep happy memories of the past alive, as long as you are intent on making more happy memories instead of hankering only after old ones.

The past can be beneficial only if we use our good memories to motivate us for the future and if we learn from our past mistakes and then forget them.

Worrying about the past, wishing for the past and depressing yourself over the events of the past is a total waste of your precious resource of time.

Dale Carnegie explained it so well when he said, *'You cannot saw sawdust! And it's the same with the past. When you start worrying about things that are over and done with, you're merely trying to saw sawdust.'*

Which category do you fall under?

People in general can be grouped into two categories – those that live in the past and are known to say things like, 'This is what I did. This is what I was. This is where I've been,' and those that live for the future and are known to say things like, ' This is what I'm going to do. This is what I'm going to be. This is where I'm going.'

Go on, read the above paragraph again! Which category do you fall into? Do you find that you are always thinking about the good old days or are you one of the few who have learnt and profited from your past as you stride confidently into the challenging future?

Chapter 2

Wasting our Precious Time

'Procrastination is the thief of time.'
Edward Young, ' Night Thoughts'

Many years ago, whilst on a long working holiday overseas with friends, we spent two months on a Moshav in Israel. This is similar to a Kibbutz set-up, where young 'volunteers' from all over the world come together to work mainly on farms in a relaxed, friendly and communal environment. We worked as farm labourers, picking, sorting and pruning various fruit.

There were two permanent Arab farm labourers who worked with us, Ali and Achmed. We chatted to Ali one day, as he seemed even more down in the dumps than usual.

Upon inquiry, Ali said, 'I feel like I am stuck here. Stuck in this place, stuck in this job and stuck with this life I don't want.'

In his eyes we saw the deep sadness of a bitter and frustrated man. Ali continued, 'You know I have worked for this farmer for 20 years. For 20 years I have worked his land day after day. Years ago when I was younger, I still dreamed of having my own land, my very own farm. But somehow it just never happened.

'Every year I would tell myself, 'Ali, this is the year', but something always came up and I would put it off, thinking that there was plenty of time and what was my hurry as I was comfortable enough for the moment. You see I have always wished for a better life, but I guess I have done nothing about it. It seems like I woke up one day and 20 years had flown by. 20 years of my life gone with nothing to show for it but lost dreams and lost time.'

Ali continued, 'I feel like my life is over already. I have had my chances and now they have run out. It is too late for me to better my situation, as I have a family and other responsibilities now, which I cannot jeopardise.'

There are so many people like Ali. People who get caught up in a rut and before they know it, time has escaped them and they've wasted years of their life. The majority of people fall into this trap either at work or in a relationship. They slip into this 'comfort zone' which is easy and tolerable at first, but quickly gets depressing and frustrating, stealing months and often years of their time.

So how do people like Ali escape the rut they have created for themselves? They can only break free from their rut by constantly trying to better themselves and their situation. They can do this without jeopardising their present security through: learning new skills, furthering their studies, setting new goals and actively working at reaching them. They alone have to promote change so that they can alter their course, escaping the deep rut they have created for themselves.

Are you stuck in a rut? Are you cruising in a 'comfort zone' and going nowhere fast? Do you wake up every morning around about the same time to get ready for the job you would rather not do? Then drive the same route to work and see the same faces every day that you would rather not see? Do you then do the same monotonous tasks every day when you would far rather be doing something else?

Perhaps you're trapped in a relationship you definitely should not be in, all the while telling yourself that you really must do something about your situation so you can be happy. But you never get around to it! You somehow never seem to find or make the time in your set routine to make changes for the better. You console yourself saying, 'It's O.K for now.' 20 years later when nothing has changed, it's not so O.K!

Stop wasting time now!

Stop wasting time! In other words, stop choosing to do the less important, but more attractive things in life when you could utilise that time to do the more important, less attractive, but more beneficial things in life! This is quite a mouthful, but what we mean is, you could start by dragging your 'zombie like' attention away from your usual four hour dose of television. Instead, do something constructive like reading, studying, working on a hobby, going to the gym, completing a report for work or fixing something in the house.

At work you could stop putting off that extremely important phone call that may be unpleasant. Do the necessary courses to develop your knowledge and skills. Or stop going on those extra long tea breaks and lunches.

The more important things in life have lasting effects and benefits while the less important things give only temporary satisfaction. So make sure you choose to do the more important things in life with long-term benefits over the less important things offering only short-term satisfaction.

The difference between those who succeed in life and those who fail, is that those who succeed always do what is most **beneficial** for them at any given moment, whether they feel like it at the time or not. In contrast, those who fail, always seem to do what is most **pleasurable** for them at any given moment, whether it is beneficial for them long-term or not.
If you want to be like the winners, you must try to spend every second

of your time doing the most important or productive thing possible. That means, going for that work out even though it is the last thing you feel like doing, approaching that person even though you may get rejected or studying tonight even though your favourite program is on TV. It means never procrastinating, never just getting by and simply plodding along and never watching the clock and wishing the day away. In a nutshell, it means doing what is necessary now to move you closer to your desired outcome.

Most importantly, you must realise that often the most beneficial thing you should do now, could be the last thing you actually feel like doing. Winners realise this and always do the most beneficial thing now, losers don't!

If you don't believe us, look around you. You will no doubt find that those who always take the easiest and often most pleasurable route in any given situation have achieved very little in the long run, often doing themselves more harm than good. All these people have to show for their squandered time is probably a life, no better, maybe even worse than before. Without realising it they are continually asking themselves, 'What can I do right now that will be most pleasurable to me?' Instead they should be continually asking themselves, 'What can I do right now that will benefit me the most in the long run?'

You will no doubt find that those who always do the most beneficial and productive thing at any given time will be rewarded with one or more of the following: good health, greater knowledge and skill, stronger relationships, increased wealth and greater self-fulfilment.

Act now!

If you make a point of doing the most important or productive thing every moment of your life, your future will take care of itself. Developing this one habit has the effect of propelling you forward, thrusting you well on your way to success. You and those around you will be awed by your amazing progress. Adopting this habit will positively affect every facet of your life. What are you waiting for?

Every second of every day, ask yourself, **'What is the most productive thing I can do right now?' and DO IT!**

If you don't **'DO IT'** then you are obviously a procrastinator. This is a bad habit you need to change if you are to achieve success.

How do you change this bad habit of procrastination? Simple! All you have to do is remember 2 words. Memorise these 2 words. Repeat them over and over, until they are burnt into your mind, forever.

What are these 2 words that can cause such a positive change in any procrastinator? **'ACT NOW!'** That's it! The moment you think of what you should be doing, repeat the words **'ACT NOW!'** to yourself, then follow immediately with positive action.

Start now. Practice this until it becomes second nature and you will find that you automatically get things done instead of putting them off for another day. You will eventually have replaced the bad habit of procrastination with the positive habit of always getting things done.

Live for today

There is only one place we can possibly live and that is in the present. But still millions of people from all walks of life do themselves untold damage by spending a large portion of their lives living in the past or in the distant future. Whenever we explain to these people the importance of living in the present we do so as follows:

Picture your mind as a vehicle travelling on a one way street called life. The road in front of you is your future and the road behind you is your past. The vehicle that is your mind cannot turn back just as you cannot live in the past. Some still try to live in the past by worrying and thinking too much about what they've left behind. This only serves to slow their progress down, as they will not be concentrating fully on controlling their vehicle in the present.

In the same respect, when you worry and think too much about the distant future, this also serves to slow your progress down and cause problems, as again you will not be concentrating fully on controlling the vehicle of your mind in the present.

The only way to prepare adequately for the sharp bends, obstacles and potholes still to come in the future is to concentrate your full attention and energy on the task at hand. **There is only one way to make the best of the future and that is to put the past behind you and make the best of today.**

Most of mankind is also in the habit of putting off living today for a better tomorrow. By all means, dream of good things to come, but you must enjoy the ride along the way. Don't wait for an age, a stage in your life or a dream to come true to really live – live now and enjoy the moment, this hour and every day of your life.

When I grow up....

When we are small children we think that things will get better when we grow up. When we are grown up we think things will get better when we get a job and earn some money. Once we have a job, we think things will get better once we have a car and a place of our own. Then we feel things will improve when we get married. Once married we feel things will get better when we retire.

In this way, throughout their lives so many people put off happiness, love, fun, feeling great about themselves and ultimately living. Then one day they look back and realise that they have missed the point of it all. They discover, too late, that life is in the living. They missed out on so much that life had to offer because they were always waiting for and dreaming of better things to come. We simply must make the best of every moment, hour and day and good things will naturally follow.

"Put off living whilst waiting for a better life and you may wait a lifetime!"
Warren Veenman & Sally Eichhorst

'Today' will never dawn again. 'Today' is a precious gift that can slip away with alarming speed. Wasted, it will eat a chunk out of your life, but lived well, it will fulfil your life and make it whole.

When I win the lotto....

We chatted to Howard, a successful businessman who hit the nail on the head, when he said that we are living in an age of instant gratification.

'People are waiting for the day they win the lotto, in order to have the money they want, to do what they want and live the lives they want.' Howard said, ' Masses of people are living for the day they win the lotto. You know there is a whole culture in the UK that plan their lives around winning the National Lottery. The day might never arrive, whilst their lives may have wasted away in the meantime.'

Isn't it amazing that so many people have this 'When I win the Lotto' psychology. Do you?

Make the time

We pointed out at the beginning of this book that you will not enjoy the maximum benefit this book has to offer unless you take the time to really read it, absorb it and understand it. All worthwhile things take time and effort. **Make the time and don't allow Time to become The Enemy...**

THE ENEMY

Time, the unknown enemy, beats its rhythmic pulse.
Unstoppable, it bulldozes ahead, crushing the life from those that delay.
'Wait, tomorrow, just now' is screamed, but alas it is too late.
Time forges on as for no man will time wait.
Time makes no promises and accepts no responsibility for a life that is rife with waste.

A man lies dying; alone, weak and cold he moans-'Time why have you deceived me-so many things unsaid, undone-where were you to see that things got done?'
His life flashes before him; every wasted moment a reminder of what may have been.
Never will tomorrow be another day as tomorrow has come all too soon and all that remains are yesterdays.

Time looks on momentarily saddened by such wasted life. So many unchallenged opportunities, meaningless relationships, uncharted territory and plans run dry.
For a fleeting moment Time recalls all those that have suffered the same fate.
Time may be the unknown enemy but man's individual choices are the KNOWN ENEMY
Sally Eichhorst

Part 2

Unleash the Infinite Power Within You

'The mind is its own place,
and in itself can make a heaven of Hell,
a hell of Heaven.'

John Milton, 'Paradise Lost'

Chapter 3

The Power of Thought

'It's not who you are that holds you back,
it's what you think you're not!

Denis Waitley

There are countless reasons why people do not succeed in life. However, there are two predominant reasons that clearly stand out from all the others.

One - **Many unsuccessful people believe that they were cheated out of success, because the world did not give them the same chances and opportunities as those who achieved success. They blame everyone and everything but themselves, believing their failures are due only to situations outside themselves.**

Listening to their reasons for not succeeding, it is highly likely that you would be subjected to some of the following excuses:

- 'I come from a poor family, so my opportunities were very limited.'
- 'My parents could not afford to pay for a proper education.'
- 'My parents got divorced and it left me unbalanced.'
- 'My father drank too much and was a bad influence on me.'
- 'I hung around with a bad crowd who led me down the wrong path.'

One need only look at people such as Stevie Wonder and Ray Charles, who despite their blindness, are extremely talented musicians. They did not hide behind their blindness as an excuse not to succeed and accomplish great things.

Two - There are others who blame their failures on the times that they are living in, adopting a totally pessimistic outlook regarding their country and the world as a whole.

Do any of these excuses sound familiar:

- 'This country is falling apart and dragging me along with it.'
- 'Increasing taxes and inflation are eating away at my stagnant salary.'
- 'The times we are living in could not be worse.'
- 'The crime rate is increasing every day along with unemployment. What happened to the good old days when there was hardly any crime, plenty of jobs and my money was worth something?'
- 'What a world we live in – the threat of war, stories of famine and atrocities against mankind.'
- ' How can you even plan ahead or be optimistic when we have the threat of nuclear warfare and environmental damage that can end the world we live in?'

Since the dawn of time there have been those who have prophesised depression, destruction and the inevitable collapse of their world. Well, the world is still here and we are pretty sure it will still be here long after you and I have departed. Every generation seems to think that they have it bad. But in essence, we have more opportunities now than we have ever had, regardless of who we are or our present situation.

What you think is what you are!

When your mind is filled with these pessimistic and negative thoughts, you are limiting your chances of ever succeeding and preventing your mind from unleashing its true capabilities.

You, regardless of race, religion, background, environment, age or sex, possess an infinite power within you that can remove any obstacle from your mind and propel you towards your ultimate desires.

With this power you can create, construct and reinforce any area of your life. What is this power we speak of? **This power is the ability to choose your own thoughts**. Think about it; your thoughts are the only thing you have total control over as no one can tell you what to think or how to think.

You simply cannot allow yourself to underestimate the importance of what you think. What you think is what you are!

Emerson said, *'A man is what he thinks about all day long.'* In other words, your thoughts make up the person you are. You couldn't possibly be anything else!

It is a fact that your daily thoughts eventually influence the person you become. For example:
If you have weak thoughts you will become a weak person.
If you have confident thoughts, you will become a confident person.
If you have strong thoughts you will become a strong person.
If you have thoughts on self- pity you will become a person filled with self- pity.
If you have loving thoughts you will become a loving person.
If you have fearful thoughts you will become a fearful person.

If you continually think about all the reasons why you will never succeed in life, you are creating a person who has all the reasons in the world not to succeed and is sure to fail.

Chapter 4

The Spreading Poison of Negative Influences

'Rediscover the child within you.
The child who can conquer the world.'
Warren Veenman & Sally Eichhorst

If it is so easy to attract success by simply focusing only on positive thoughts and actions, then why do so many people still not succeed in life?

The answer lies in man's common weakness of exposing his mind to the negative influences of others. This negative influence takes root from an early age, spreading its poison as the years unfold, like the weeds in a neglected garden.

The little entrepreneur

Let's examine this idea more closely. When you were a child and the weather was cold and rainy, how did you feel? I'll bet you were brimming with excitement at the thought of splashing in the puddles and playing in the mud. Maybe you enjoyed sitting, cosy, warm and secure indoors, whilst listening to the falling rain. If it snowed, you were probably even more overjoyed at the prospect of building a snowman, enjoying a snowball fight or dad teaching you how to ski or skate. The possibilities of adventure and fun, whether snowy, rainy or sunny were endless.

If you were a child waking up to rainy or snowy weather, chances are the weatherman, mom, dad or other grown ups would be grumbling and complaining endlessly about what a miserable day this was going to be. The weatherman was probably announcing the following in his most grave and solemn voice, 'Sorry to be the bearer of bad news, but unfortunately it's a bad weather day with plenty of rain. To add to the already miserable day and worsen the situation, some areas may also encounter snowfalls. This troublesome cold front will worsen as the week progresses.'

When you're a child the day looks pretty great until the weatherman's report of doom and gloom changes your mood, or mom, dad and other grown-ups have their say about the 'miserable' day. When you're a child you never complain about the weather until others influence and teach you otherwise. Likewise as a child, everything in life looks positive. You feel you can conquer the world, achieve the impossible, embark on adventures, believe wholeheartedly in yourself, feel you can be and do anything you desire and love all kinds of weather – that is until you are told otherwise, forever influencing your thoughts and beliefs.

It is a fact that at least 8 out of 10 children entering Nursery School or Class 1, start out feeling good about themselves. This means that more than 80% of us begin our lives feeling good about ourselves. Sadly as children get older, the number who still feel the same way drops drastically. As they become teenagers the number decreases even more.

Who steals our self worth?

What is shocking and proven by studies, is that more than 75% of adults suffer from low self worth. Can you believe it? Only 1 in 4 adults feel good about themselves. Between the ages of 5 years and early adulthood most of us experience a diminishing self worth. What happens along the way to create such a loss?

Irrespective of who we are, we are all born with a clean and positive slate that is our minds. At this stage we are unaware of what is right or wrong, good or evil and what we can or cannot do. However, with time, like a sponge, our minds absorb influences from everything and everyone around us.

Up until a school going age, the majority of young children are only exposed to the negative influences of family. So until they start their schooling, most kids still view themselves as winners, sure of themselves and their capabilities. Once they have started school and progress through the years, they are far more vulnerable to the negative influences of others – no longer only family, but now also teachers, friends, television, media and books. As they become inundated with negative influences, they tend to lose confidence in themselves becoming unsure of their abilities and self worth.

If, as a child you are enriched with positive influences and you are convinced that you have the capacity to achieve great things, then it is highly likely that you will achieve great things as an adult, no matter what challenges or setbacks are thrown at you.

It is our aim to help you rediscover the child within you and to show you that you have the capacity to achieve great things no matter what your past or present circumstances.

Chapter 5

The Hidden World of the Subconscious

'Our life is what our thoughts make it.'
Marcus Aurelius, 'Meditations'

You may not be aware of it, but you are forever existing in two overlapping worlds: your subconscious world consisting of your thoughts, feelings and attitudes and your conscious world consisting of the people, places and circumstances you come across in your life. Your subconscious is a powerful tool, which has and will always influence every part of your life. It is the most vital part of who and what you are, and will ultimately determine whether you succeed or fail.

Opposing forces doing battle

How does the subconscious hold such power, causing you to succeed or fail? The answer lies in the two great powers the subconscious wields, the power to attract success and the power to repel success.

Think back! Haven't you had days when everything went wrong? From the moment you got up and spilled coffee on your new suit, followed by the car not starting, then the endless traffic jam and to top it all your disastrous day at work. Then there are those days that everything goes your way and it seems you can do no wrong.

Well, you're the same person, doing the same thing, so what causes you to fall flat one day and become a champion the next day? What causes even the most successful candidates in the world to have days when they excel at everything and then have days when everything they do is wrong?

The answer lies in the constant conflict between the two great powers of the subconscious. These two forces are continually fighting for dominance and your state of mind on any particular day depends upon which one is dominant.

On the one side you have PMA (Positive Mental Attitude) and on the other side you have NMA (Negative Mental Attitude). The one can attract the life you want: money, power, prestige, health, happiness and fame. The other can repel all these things.

It is a Positive Mental Attitude that makes it possible for men to reach the pinnacle of their dreams and it is a Negative Mental Attitude that keeps others wallowing at the bottom, never rising and amounting to anything.

When your mind is dominated with thoughts of hate, jealousy, worry, envy etc. you create for yourself a Negative Mental Attitude. When your mind is dominated with thoughts of love, sincerity, optimism, faith, courage, generosity, hope, ambition, confidence, initiative etc. you create for yourself a Positive Mental Attitude.

So take care and be aware when using your mind, that your ability to succeed in everything you do, relies on you creating a mind dominated by positive thoughts.

Adopt P.M.A. (Positive mental Attitude)

The adoption of a Positive Mental Attitude is of extreme importance if you are to enjoy success in any area of your life as it influences everything you do.

People who succeed seem to gain access to this positive state on a consistent basis. Those who soar amongst the winners are masters when it comes to tapping into that part of their mind, which promotes all their positive and empowering qualities.

To develop a mind that is dominated by positive thoughts, you should always be aware of what thoughts you are feeding your mind. This can be done by focusing on what you want from life and not on what you don't want.

If you continually focus on what you want from life, you put yourself in a positive state, which will attract all these things to you.

> *'Fill your mind with positive thoughts.*
> *Fill your world with positive people.*
> *Then you will fill your Life with all you want.'*
> **Warren Veenman & Sally Eichhorst**

Protect your internal 'computer' from viruses

What people don't realise is that the subconscious is like a powerful computer that never sleeps and is constantly absorbing information without you being aware of it. For example, those adverts that are repeated over and over on the TV, at the movies or on the radio – We suppose you think you are far too smart for them to have any affect on you? Wrong! It doesn't matter what you see or hear, whether you consciously believe it or not, when vividly repeated often enough, it does affect you. It influences your thoughts and beliefs about that product, with or without your awareness and whether you want it to or not. Your subconscious accepts this information about the product as true. It thus forms beliefs about this product, which influences the subsequent actions you will take.

So you should be extremely protective about what you allow to penetrate your subconscious mind. If your subconscious mind has absorbed continual thoughts of fear, it will accept these thoughts as true and make them beliefs. The danger here is that the subconscious will then get to work to make them a reality, attracting those very situations or things you fear. This is a fact! What is held in your subconscious mind and the experiences you face in your life are most definitely closely inter-linked.

If you are determined to focus your thoughts repetitively on the bad things in life, painting a picture of future doom and gloom in your mind, then be prepared to fulfil your own negative forecast with frightening and hair-raising accuracy. If instead, you paint an optimistic picture of hope, courage and all the good things in life, then expect to attract these things to you.

The untapped power of your mind

It is said that most of us use less than 10 % of our brain capacity, yet we are still capable of achieving incredible things. We are all destined for greatness, but it is up to us to realise this potential and derive the maximum benefit from our given gift – our minds.

If most of us use less than 10% of our brain capacity, what is the purpose of the other 90%? We doubt very much that it was meant to simply fill in space. Surely it is there for a reason as is everything in our bodies?

What wonders we could all achieve if only we could believe so deeply in ourselves and be able to tap into the unused areas of our mind?

The remarkable and limitless power of the subconscious goes beyond what we consider to be normal and possible. As unbelievable as it seems, you can direct your subconscious to bring you the things you want from life.

It is our aim in this book to open the door to your mind, tapping into the tremendous potential that lies dormant therein.

Chapter 6

You are what you think!

'Masters of self-communication have mastered their lives.'
Warren Veenman & Sally Eichhorst

Self thoughts

You may not be aware of it, but you talk to yourself all the time and what you say to yourself has a strong influence on who and what you are, as it affects your actions, behaviour and decisions.

What others say to you or think of you has little affect on your wellbeing, when compared to the opinion you have of yourself and what you say to yourself. You may experience outward success in the form of money, fame and status, but to experience the inward success most of us long for, such as happiness, love and prosperity, you must become a master at communicating with yourself.

It is as though we have this jukebox inside our head, which is playing non-stop. The records consist of all the feelings we are capable of, good or bad. These include belief, worry, desire, anger, fear, frustration, happiness, hope etc. Depending upon the situation we encounter, we select a record and play it over and over to ourselves.

Becoming a master at self-communication

You can start by making a pact with yourself that from this moment on, you will stop moaning and wallowing in self- pity and quit criticising and judging yourself too harshly.

When you mentally repeat to yourself, 'stupid fool,' or 'I can't do it,' or feed your mind with words like worthless, ugly, stupid, dumb, it eventually becomes a belief in your subconscious and you will start behaving like this.

So be aware the next time you scold yourself and put a stop to it immediately. Remember your subconscious will give you exactly what you want. So, if you feed your mind with negative input about yourself, it will accept this as the truth and promote such behaviour until you decide to change the messages you are feeding it.

A further word of advice is that your subconscious does not have a sense of humour, so don't joke about yourself negatively. As we discussed earlier, your mind does not know the difference between something that is imagined and something that is real, so it will take you seriously.

Take control of your mental 'jukebox'

So from now on when you talk to yourself use words like 'I can do it, I'm the best' and watch the difference in all that you do.

In a nutshell, to become a master at self-communication, you need to retrain yourself to think and speak positively. You need to realise that what you put in, is what you get out. Make it a daily habit to use self-talk to benefit you in your every day life.

Remember that you cannot stop the 'jukebox' from playing a record, but you can choose the desired record. If you are not selective about the records you choose and allow any old one to play, it may not be the one that will enhance you. Be selective of the messages you play over and over to yourself, making sure that they build you up rather than put you down.

Think of some positive things you can say about yourself now. Don't wait a second longer. Start now!

Pat on the back

Can you recall the last time you accomplished something great? How did it make you feel? Were you excited, motivated, proud as a peacock? Maybe you felt you could conquer the world and were unstoppable?

Whatever you felt we bet you couldn't help thinking about it for a few days afterwards! Sadly, this wonderful feeling wears off all too soon as we become wrapped up in our daily work and play. Sometimes these memories become so distant that we even forget that we accomplished them at all.

Unfortunately most of us are experts when it comes to finding fault with ourselves rather than recognising and maintaining pride in our accomplishments.

So instead of focusing on your weaknesses and failures, rather praise yourself as often as possible for your past and present successes. This will create within you the positive energy you need to reach your present goal.

It is imperative that you regularly spend a few minutes focusing on your past successes, no matter how long ago they occurred. This will serve to provide a renewed boost of energy that will help you to achieve success again and again and can have a formidable impact in all areas of your life.

Remember, success attracts success and the more it attracts, the stronger and more powerful its force. When you focus on all your positive qualities, as well as your past and present achievements, you are guaranteed to attract success.

Stop reminding yourself about your weaknesses and rather celebrate your strengths. Feel proud and wonderful about yourself and your achievements, never letting any of your victories fade away to be lost and forgotten. Do it now and every day!

Chapter 7

The secret to controlling your thoughts

'Seize control of your mind now so that you may live the life you choose and not the life that it chooses for you.'
Warren Veenman & Sally Eichhorst

You are now aware that you have the power to control your thoughts and if used correctly this can benefit you in every area of your life.

To illustrate more clearly how your mind operates we would like you to compare it to the producer of a motion picture. If the producer wants to produce a sad reaction from his audience, he would choose suitably melancholy music and create an altogether depressing and dreary scene. If he wants to scare you, he would bring in the appropriate sounds, frightening scenes and horrific footage. What if he wanted to make a happy movie? He would change the scene with bright, colourful lighting, light hearted music and jovial faces.

If the producer wanted a scene to make the audience feel good, motivated and uplifted he would bring in the appropriate sights and sounds leaving them feeling great.

You are the producer in charge of your mind, so you have the power to set any scene you desire. Just as the movie producer is in total control of what you see, hear and feel, you are similarly in total control of the thoughts entering and leaving your mind.

You can skilfully brighten, enlarge and increase the affect of the positive messages in your mind, just as you can diminish and fade out the negative messages.

Unfortunately most people do not exercise this control as they do not know how to go about it and are often unaware of the incredibly positive effects it can have.

> *It is the power of the mind that can make rich from poor,*
> *happy from sad and health from sickness.*
> **WARREN VEENMAN & SALLY EICHHORST**

To teach you to take control of your mind, we have designed two tasks.

These tasks will show you:

> **Firstly**, how you can transform your state of mind to be instantaneously positive and empowering, enabling you to attract the things you want from life.

> **Secondly**, how you can remove all negative and limiting thoughts from your mind for good.

Task 1

By following this simple exercise, we aim to show you through using one or more of your 5 senses of sight, sound, taste, smell and touch, how to manipulate your thoughts at will and transform your state of mind to a positive one.

This exercise should take less than 5 minutes and can be done wherever and whenever you feel the need to motivate, inspire or lift yourself from a negative state.

Firstly, find a quiet place where you won't be disturbed for about 5 minutes. Now close your eyes and relax.

Think about something really wonderful that happened to you – it could be anything that made you feel happy, proud, loved or any of the other desired, positive states. It does not matter how far back you stretch your memory as long as you can easily retrieve the image.

Now take this image and bring it closer to you. Brighten the image as if painting it with splashes of lively colours, making it stand out until it almost comes alive. Make the voices louder and intensify the feelings that go with this image.

Now magnify the image, making it so large that it seems to fill every inch of your mind. It should be bigger, brighter and closer to you than ever before.

Notice how your feelings intensify when you do this. When you make this image bigger and brighter, you increase the power and feelings of this image and it puts you in a much more enjoyable mood or state.

Now take that same image and push it away from you, turning down the sound and dimming the colours. Watch it get smaller and smaller. You will notice that the intensified pleasant feelings you recently felt, have started to dissolve as the image moves further away and begins to fade. Notice how easily you can manipulate this image, making it as powerful or as weak as you like.

Now, think of something gloomy, hurtful or distressing that happened to you. It could be something in your past or present, that still causes you pain whenever you think about it.

Now brighten this unpleasant memory. Also magnify it and move it closer and closer towards you. Make any sounds and voices louder. What happens now? Notice how all the bad and negative feelings related to this incident come flooding back and are even more intense and painful than ever.

Now take this same unpleasant image and make it smaller and smaller, shrinking it until you can barely see it. How are you feeling now? Notice how this feeling has lost its power over you, like a once powerful and destructive flame being doused into a mere flicker. Now make this image even smaller. Then make it all fuzzy and hard to see. Now turn all sounds down and see yourself pushing this image away. Keep pushing it away and watch it fade into the distance until it disappears altogether from your world. You will be amazed to find that those negative and depressing feelings you experienced have also faded and disappeared.

From this exercise, it is evident that you possess the ability to control your mind effectively. In less than 5 minutes you took a negative feeling and sapped it of its power over you. Likewise you also took a positive feeling and enhanced it, thus strengthening and empowering you.

From this moment on, you are in control of your mind. Don't let your brain decide what picture, sound or feeling it should show you. You decide how you are going to feel and take control. If you have negative images that bring you down, drain them of their power and strength and fade them into oblivion.

You can use this exercise every day of your life. It is especially effective when you are faced with disturbing memories that haunt you and limit your present potential. In your mind's eye you can fade out these memories and instead, enhance your good memories.

In the same way you can also shrink large ominous tasks or problems, making them less overbearing and more approachable. In this way you will be far more likely to complete the task or overcome the problem, as you will feel far more capable and confident now that it no longer looms over you like a giant hurdle.

Task 2

In this simple exercise we are going to show you how to remove negative thoughts from your mind for good.

Starting today, for only half an hour, all that we want you to do is not to think of one negative thought. That's it! For half an hour, think only of strong, powerful and positive thoughts. When a negative thought tries to creep in (and it will), gently direct your mind back to a positive thought.

After one week, increase this half an hour exercise to one hour. Every week thereafter, keep increasing the time spent on this exercise by another hour, until you are spending the entire day concentrating on only thinking positive thoughts.

Remember that your mind will attract anything that it continuously dwells upon. So when you have reached the level when you can go a whole day, eradicating almost all negative thoughts and dwelling only on positives, your ultimate desires will almost effortlessly be attracted to you.

What we have found works wonders for us when we do this exercise, is that whenever a negative thought intrudes, trying to bring us down and pull us away from our goals, we say the word 'rubbish bin' silently to ourselves. We see this negative image being thrown into a garbage can and the lid being shut tight.

After using this approach for a number of days, we found that when negative thoughts attempted to intrude, it was as though this word (rubbish bin) was standing guard at the door of our minds. It seemed to automatically appear at the same time as any negative thought, removing it before it could have any affect.

We found that with time, it became difficult to even think of a negative thought. Remember that positive and negative thoughts cannot occupy the mind at the same time. By regularly making sure that only positive thoughts dominate your mind, it will eventually become a habit and your mind will at some stage become so dominantly positive that negatives will simply be unable to enter.

'Feed your mind with the right, positive thoughts.
Protect your mind from the wrong, negative thoughts.
Now prepare yourself for unimaginable rewards.'
Warren Veenman & Sally Eichhorst

Your mind can be likened to a garden and you are the gardener. You have two choices: you can either plant the right seeds, remove all the weeds, landscape the garden and protect it from pests and the elements. Or you can ignore it, leaving it vulnerable to grow as it will, leaving itself open and unprotected from pests and the elements. Whatever you do, one thing is certain, you will get out only as much as you are willing to put in.

Make no mistake, your garden will grow, whether you decide to look after it or not, but it may not be what you want. To reap the rewards of a beautiful and well kept garden you must be prepared to put in the necessary effort. So make the effort every day to feed your mind with positive thoughts and protect it from negative thoughts and you will reap unimaginable rewards.

Part 3

Conquer the Mental Obstacles that Limit You!

'As he thinketh in his heart, so is he'

Proverbs 23:7

Chapter 8

Stop Worrying!

'Little things affect little minds.'
Benjamin Disraeli, 'Sybil'

Gareth T Millwright is a happily married man running a very successful business importing leather goods. Nothing seems to get him down, least of all worries. He seems to have a permanent smile on his face and always comes across as positive and motivated. 'I wasn't always like this.' Gareth explained to us.

'When I first started my own business, I used to worry about everything. Would I make enough money to live every month? Would my creditors close me down? Would my business be successful? Would my leather imports arrive on time? It wasn't only my new business that I worried about. I worried about everything. I worried whether or not I was correctly dressed and socially acceptable. I worried that I may never meet someone to love and to settle down with. I worried that I was getting old. I worried that my car may pack in at any time. I even worried that I may get sick and would be unable to run my business.'

Gareth laughed as he continued, ' I simply could not stop worrying and would sometimes work myself into an absolute state, driving myself and those around me crazy. I can't believe how much time and energy I wasted soaking up all these worries. I felt I was constantly on the verge of a nervous breakdown. Worrying used to eat a big chunk out of my existence. Some nights I never slept at all because of worry.'

Smiling, looking totally relaxed and a far cry from a nervous breakdown, Gareth continued, 'One day I decided, 'Enough is enough!' I had to do something before worry totally destroyed me. So I did something quite simple, but unbelievably effective. Every day from that day on, I wrote down at the bottom of my diary exactly what was worrying me on that particular day. Every Sunday evening, I would then page back in my diary and review the entire week's worries. I knew what people had said to me about the majority of our worries never materialising, but now I had proved it for myself. Of the worries I was constantly writing down, 99% never happened. All that worrying for nothing!

'Now I don't know the meaning of the word worry because I've realised that there is a 99% chance that my worries will never become a reality. Now I don't waste my time and energy worrying about something until it happens. Just this small change has created a major improvement in all areas of my life. Family and friends can't believe I'm even the same person!'

Gareth realised that most of what he worried about came from his imagination and not from his physical existence. If any one of us had to look back over the years, we too would realise that most of our worries were also only a figment of our imagination.

Imagine that! Over 99% of the things we worry about never happen. Think about it; less than one percent of the things we worry about may actually happen. But still we worry about everything.

Even more ridiculous is what people actually worry about! Do we worry and have sleepless nights about very real and major things in life? Do we worry about contracting A.I.D.S., that silent and dangerous killer? Do we worry about subjecting our bodies to the threat of heart attacks, strokes, cancer and other life threatening ailments caused by smoking, drinking, poor eating habits and lack of exercise? Are we worried about being caught up in a 3rd World War with possible nuclear implications, or the drastic environmental damage we are inflicting on our World? What about worrying whether we will become yet another of the statistics to be involved in a car accident?

These are substantial worries indeed, but instead, everyone is losing sleep over their own little unfounded worries, which will probably never materialise. If by some remote chance these worries become a reality, they would in most cases not result in dire consequences. One would think that people would worry about more important things, which have a high probability of happening and could have drastic outcomes. The point is that if you're going to worry about trivialities, then rather not worry at all!

We are not saying that you should only worry about major events. We are just using these examples to help you put your worries in true perspective. We often face major catastrophes in life fearlessly but then let trivial things pull us down.

Put worry into better perspective

Jenna Armstrong helps put worry into better perspective by sharing a near fatal experience she had.

'It all happened so quickly,' remarked Jenna. 'One minute I was racing along in my car, rushing to get to a meeting. Next thing I knew, I was lying upside down in a shallow stream. I could see the water slowly enveloping my car and watched it seeping in. Then the water reached me, icy cold against my skin. My seat belt was stuck and my legs were trapped. The more I struggled, the more panicked and disorientated I became.

'I was going to drown! I gave up struggling as if accepting the inevitable. My life flashed before me. Just a few moments ago I had been worried about not arriving at my meeting on time. I had also been worried about whether the presentation I had prepared for the meeting was good enough, whether I looked presentable enough and whether these potential clients would like me. It was these worries which had landed me in this predicament.'

Jenna shuddered as she recalled her last thoughts before passing out, 'It suddenly dawned on me that I was a constant worrier. I worried about reaching my target at work, my boss who I felt didn't like me, the work I didn't really like, the clothes I couldn't really afford, whether my curtains matched my duvet, not having enough money at the end of each month and not having a fantastic pension scheme. I even worried about a new spot on my face and a little weight I had gained.'

Jenna sighed deeply and continued, 'How important and massive these worries seemed at the time. How small and insignificant they were now, as I lay trapped upside down in a sea of water. Before I passed out, I vowed that if by some miracle I was saved from the clutches of death, I would never again waste the precious time and energy I had left on fruitless worries. I would never let worry get the better of me again.'

Jenna was saved by a passer-by who managed to free her from the water-logged vehicle. Miraculously she escaped serious injury. 'I have a new lease on life and I certainly won't waste even a second of it worrying about silly, unfounded trivialities. I have realised now that life is too short and time is too precious to waste on worrying.'

Often it is only when something major happens in our lives, that we become aware of just how short our time here can be. So don't waste your precious time and energy on worrying. It simply isn't worth it!

How to avoid worry!

When we are busy at work with our mind full of the challenges of the day, it is difficult for the 'worry bug' to creep in. It is when the mind is free from the day's work and we are doing nothing in particular or lying in bed with the lights out that the 'worry bug' has its chance to creep in. We may worry about things that have gone wrong during the day, what we shouldn't have said to our spouse or whether we are getting anywhere in life.

So how do you avoid worrying? Simple! An excellent way to avoid worrying is to allow yourself no time for worrying. In other words, keep your mind occupied. Every human mind can only think of one thing at a time. (We explore this fact further in Part 4) Hence, a busy and occupied mind leaves no space or time for worry.

When you are busy at work, engrossed in hobbies like painting or reading, playing a sport of some sort or involved in a charitable cause far bigger than yourself, you have no time to brood or worry.

What we find does wonders for ridding us of the 'worry bug' is to read a few chapters of a motivational book every evening before we go to bed. Now that really implants the right positive thoughts in our minds before we drift off to sleep! So try it!

Destroying the 'worry bug'

We have come up with a short step-by-step plan to help you eliminate the majority of your worries. We recommend that you start with one worry at a time until they are all where they belong – buried and forgotten, never to surface again. One word of warning! Don't try to answer these questions without writing them down. When you write the question and answer down you will find that it helps clarify your thinking.

Step 1. Write down a clear and precise statement of exactly what it is that is worrying you.
For example, 'I am worried that my performance at work is not good enough.'

Step 2. Now decide whether or not this thing is really worth worrying about.
In other words, ask yourself, 'Why am I worrying about this and is it really worth worrying about?' For example, 'Yes, it is worth worrying about as I could lose my job if my superiors also believe that my performance is really not good enough.' If you find that you are worried about something totally out of your control, such as your age or height, you must accept that there is nothing you can do about it and stop worrying about it now. Things that cannot possibly have any lasting or major influence on your life are also not worth worrying about.

Step 3. **If you have decided that it is not worth worrying about, then stop and go back to Step 1. Now write down another, more 'worthwhile' worry. If on the other hand, you have decided that it is indeed worth worrying about, then write down a list of the things you can do about it.**

This list must become your plan of action to rid yourself of this worry. It is usually the failure to arrive at this point that drives most people to worrying themselves into an early grave. You will find that once you have a plan to follow, it will feel as though a weight has been lifted off your shoulders. For example, 'I will get more work done in a day', 'I will be more flexible and helpful at work', 'I will study further in my field',' I will approach my boss and ask his opinion about my performance and how I could improve upon it.'

Step 4. **Start now to carry out your plan.**

Do something today, however small to carry out your plan. It is great that you know what it is that is worrying you. It's fantastic that you have a plan to rid yourself of this worry. But it's worthless if you don't carry it out!

'What am I worrying about?'

Most people who have achieved success in any area of their lives have learnt the benefit of replacing worry with self-confidence, encouragement and constructive thoughts. They do not waste their time and energy on trivial worries. They make firm decisions and take immediate action, avoiding lingering too long on a problem and allowing worry to surface.

Stop right now and ask yourself, 'What am I worrying about? Is this thing I'm worrying about really worth the stress it is giving me?' Chances are you'll probably find that it's something trivial and unimportant.

In most cases ninety five percent of the things in our lives are wonderful. So if you want to be happy, with a life free of worry, all you need do is focus on the ninety five percent that is great and ignore the five percent that is wrong.

Chapter 9

Fear!

' A life dominated by fear is a life half- lived.'
Warren Veenman & Sally Eichhorst

A baby is born. In its innocence, it knows no fear because it knows no better. It has not yet faced the challenge of brutal reality.

As the infant grows, many are guilty of imprinting fear on its mind.
'Behave yourself, or you'll embarrass us and people will stare.'
'Don't touch, or I'll smack.'
'If you misbehave, I'll go home without you.'
'If you're naughty, the 'boogie man' will get you.'
'Don't touch, you'll get hurt.'
'You're not clever enough to do it.'
'You clumsy fool.'
'You haven't got what it takes.'

These are just some of the often unintentionally damaging phrases blurted out by parents, family and friends, but are common in most children's upbringings. Phrases like these introduce fear and limitations into an otherwise adventurous, imaginative and often entrepreneurial mind.

Observe most young children and it will become clear that they are brilliant and creative thinkers, hungry for knowledge, new experiences and new friends. Everyday, they face the unknown head-on as they learn, smell, taste, see and hear new things, breathing and taking in all life has to offer.

If a baby was born with a fear of failure, criticism, rejection or disappointment, it may never walk, never talk and never thirst for knowledge or attempt to learn new skills. A child's innocence is its key to self-growth.

As we grow older, our fears grow too. Some of us are even encouraged and taught not to take risks, becoming afraid of challenges and a loss of security. These same people would argue that they have become wiser with age. Is this really the case? If you never take any risks you will never reap the fruitful benefits and rewards usually attached. If you become complacent and fear change, you will crumble in the face of any challenge and will never truly enjoy self-fulfilment.

When you are filled with fear, you are like a Japanese Bonsai tree, which is trimmed continuously, thereby limiting it from growing to its full potential.

Different fears

We all experience certain fears at sometime or another and some of us are much more prone to fearful thoughts than others. In order to combat this limiting negative emotion, you must first find out what it is you fear. Only then can you take steps to rid yourself of it.

There are numerous people who blame various types of fear for limiting their lives. We plan to discuss some of the most common and damaging of these fears.

Fear of loss of security, change and risk

We had just completed an interview with someone who had achieved phenomenal success and were enjoying a much deserved cup of tea with her. Her father Carl, joined us. He had recently been retrenched and was staying with her.

We started chatting to him and he said, 'You know, when I look back, I realise that I've missed out on so much. If I could have my life over again, I would definitely do things differently.'

We asked him to explain what he meant and he continued, ' Well, I realise now, that the one reason I never achieved much, is because of fear.'

'I remember when I left school, some of my close friends were going to travel and see the world. Not me! I could get a job with a strong, secure company. I feared going overseas with hardly any security and nothing to come back to. You know two of my buddies never came back. They are now running their own restaurant on the beach somewhere in Australia. The last I heard, they were opening another restaurant.'

Carl sighed, 'I always promised myself that I would eventually see the world but of course, fear killed that dream for me too. A couple of years ago, another friend of mine wanted me to go into business with him. I thought about it for a mere 5 minutes and then told him he was crazy. At least I knew that I was guaranteed of a set salary at the end of every month. Even if the salary wasn't great and I didn't really enjoy what I was doing, at least I knew I could afford to have a roof over my head and put food on the table. You see, I feared the loss of security and taking what seemed such a major risk.'

We listened further as he said, 'You know, his new business is thriving and I could just kick myself. I even turned down a number of promotions. Again fear. I feared change. I feared a new town. I feared the new people I would have to work with. I feared the added responsibilities. Yes, I even feared being criticised in case I did not succeed. You see I felt secure here with my job, my home and the town I lived in. So what happened? All the guys younger than me took the promotions that should have been mine and they eventually became my seniors.

'Before I knew it, I had been in the same company and in the same position for over 30 years. What did I get for it? What did I get in return for my fear of change, taking risks and loss of security? A retrenchment package! If only I had not let fear take over my life.'

Is Carl's problem unique? We don't think so! There are millions of people like Carl. People who have realised too late that it is fear which has doomed them to accept a life they would rather not have had. Fear held them back from what they really wanted from life by stifling any ambition that they ever had.

These people fear change because the results are unknown and may be negative. They fear taking risks as they fear failure. They fear failure as they fear the loss of security. Thus we see how closely interconnected our fears are. Like a vicious circle, they stifle our adventurous spirit and create a barrier to change, challenge and risks.

Think about Carl. He has been in the same job for 30 years doing exactly the same thing. What experience and knowledge does he have? Some would say 30 years experience and knowledge, but the real answer is one year, 30 times repeated. To grow in knowledge and experience there must be change. His fear of change created a barrier to self-growth and self-betterment.

Unfortunately most of us fear loss much more than we desire gain. Most of us work much harder hanging for dear life onto what we already have, maintaining our present standards. We do this, rather than taking risks to get what we really and truly want from our lives, thereby raising our standards. To succeed, we must learn to overcome this fear of loss. We have to realise that there is no true security in anything. If we want a better life, we have to take our chances. We must make a decision to stop fearing loss and to start focusing on what it is we want from life.

Fear of rejection

Alan is a decent, healthy and pleasant young man. He has a good job, car and home. Due to his friendly nature, he also has a close circle of friends.

'There is one major thing missing in my life,' says Alan. 'For years I have longed for just this one thing to make my life complete – the right woman to come along!'

Alan continued, 'The thing is, I have often seen women I have been interested in from a distance, but lack the nerve to approach them. Sometimes I am even introduced to the woman or know her, but I just cannot work up the courage to ask her out. The truth is, I would rather not make a move in case I am rejected.'

Alan fears rejection more than anything. It is this fear which has kept him single for numerous years and which has probably resulted in a number of the 'right women' slipping through his fingers.

'I am in my forties now,' Alan remarked, ' and I still haven't found the right woman. I still want a wife and kids, but I realise that time is no longer on my side. I know what my problem is and I wish that I could go back in time and approach all those women I feared would reject me in the hope of finding the right one.'

The wish to go back in time will do Alan no good. It simply won't happen! He must learn to eliminate his fear of rejection, and only then may he find 'Miss Right.' Good luck Alan!

That frightening word – 'No'

You simply must teach yourself to handle rejection without taking it personally. As crazy as it may sound, most of us miss out on countless opportunities because we fear the little word 'no'. The word 'no' cannot physically hurt you; it can only affect you if you allow it to.

How many times have you and will you still avoid certain things because of your fear of rejection? That attractive person you wanted to approach but didn't. That excellent job opportunity you should have applied for but didn't. The local soccer try-outs you could have gone for but didn't. The new business call you should have done but didn't. All because you were afraid of that harmless little word 'no'. Isn't it absurd that we limit ourselves in this way? What we are doing is limiting our own lives! Sure, no one enjoys rejection, but if you don't try you will never grow and never gain what you truly want from life.

Success in any area of our lives always carries with it an initial element of rejection. Rejection allows us to learn and makes us stronger.

Make a decision not to fear rejection, rather focusing on what you want from life. After all you have nothing to lose. The answer could be 'yes' or 'no' – if 'yes', then great! – if 'no', then you can always try again later and you will have learnt from your previous experience to make a better job of it next time. Remember that rejection is merely a stepping stone to most accomplishments.

Fear of criticism

'No one can make you feel inferior without your consent'
Eleanor Roosevelt

Is it not sad that there are so many out there, who permit family, friends and the general public to influence them to such an extent that they never live their lives as they truly want to. They allow these people to make decisions for them, because they fear criticism.

There are those who don't study further for a better or belated education because they may fail and fear the criticism that may follow. There are millions who won't try for a new and more prospective job, accept a promotion or take any chance in business, because they fear they may be criticized if they fail.

Some will even remain in a failed and unhappy marriage for the rest of their lives rather than face possible criticism from family and friends. We know of countless people who even keep their goals in life small and mediocre because they fear that those close to them might think they're crazy if they aim too high.

This fear of criticism does untold harm, stealing one's initiative, curbing one's imagination, breaking down one's self-confidence and hiding one's individual spirit. It is often our closest family members who criticise us the most and build inferiority complexes within us that often last a lifetime.

Any good leader of mankind must know that it is not criticism, but rather constructive suggestion, encouragement and praise that brings out the best in us. Criticism only instils fear in the human mind – fear that holds us back from trying what we would really like to do, instead of allowing others to make major decisions for us.

Remember this: if you fear criticism you will never live the life of your dreams; but only the life that others would have you live. Make a decision now to forget about what your family, friends and neighbours would think. It is not their life; it is yours. So make your own decisions based on what you really want from life.

Realise also that 99% of the time, people are thinking about themselves and not about you. They are infinitely more concerned about their own minor toothache than they are about any major event in your life.

Fear of old age and time passing you by

Jenny is a 65 year old grandmother of 4. A grandmother in the true sense of the word - loving, caring, understanding and well loved by all. She has not a care in the world and welcomes each new day with excited anticipation.

'It wasn't always this way,' Jenny recalls. ' Believe it or not, I was one of those people who was always terrified of growing old and time passing me by. Not only did I fear losing my youthful appearance with age but I also dreaded the coming of each new day. I felt time was flying by all too quickly and I would never be able to do all the things I wanted to before I grew old.

'The thought of becoming a bothersome burden, all bitter and wrinkled with nothing to do all day was a frightening thought. These fearful thoughts occupied my mind for most of the days during my youth. What a silly fool I was!

'I had painted the most awful picture of old age, turning a natural process of life into a nightmare. Now I look back on all the years I wasted worrying about and fearing the inevitable. I may be retired, grey and have wrinkles, but so do all my friends and none of us feel particularly old. If anything I'm happier now than I have ever been and I have just as much fun as I ever did. If there is one thing I have learnt in this life, it is that age has nothing to do with anything. I can still do anything I want to and believe me, I still plan to do a lot.'

Jenny concluded, ' If I could go back and change one major thing in my life, it would be to eliminate my fear of growing old and time passing me by. I wish that I had spent my younger years feeding my mind on more constructive thoughts, which would have made my life a lot more fun. I also would have welcomed and enjoyed birthdays, instead of awaiting them with frightful anticipation. Yes, if I could go back I would definitely have squashed my fear of old age, making sure that I made the best of every second in my life.'

There are so many of us that fear growing old and time passing us by. We try everything from clothing, creams and operations to keep from looking old. But growing old is as natural as life itself. We have to realize that no matter who we are, how much money we have or how beautiful and famous we may be, we are going to grow old. So why not accept it and enjoy our stay.

No one wants to look back with regret and wish they had done more, seen more and been more. So make that decision to make the best of your time here. Age is a state of mind. We don't grow old merely by a number of years. It is all in the mind. We can remain young at heart forever.

One of the most important advantages of aging, is that what we accumulate in years, we make up for in wisdom.

It is a known fact that the average person only reaches the peak of his or her success between the ages of forty and sixty. So never approach these years with fear, rather approach them with optimism and enthusiastic expectancy.

E.R.A.S.E. your fear

If you want to 'erase' your fears so that they no longer limit you from achieving your true potential, we recommend that you follow our 5-point plan. Simply follow the 5 steps below by remembering the word E.R.A.S.E.

1. **Establish what it is you fear.**
2. **Reasons for wanting to rid yourself of this fear.**
3. **Arrive at the decision to rid yourself of this fear.**
4. **Start from this moment on to take steps toward ridding yourself of this fear.**
5. **End result of expelling your fear.**

For example:
If you fear rejection, whether from the opposite sex or in sales, you would:

1. **Establish what it is you fear** – you would have to admit to yourself and accept that this fear has a dominating influence over you.
For example,
'I fear approaching someone I find attractive in case I get rejected.'
'I fear calling on certain clients in case they turn me down.'

2. **Reasons for wanting to rid yourself of this fear** – write down a list of the damage this fear has already inflicted and the

damage it will still cause in your life.

For example,

'I will never meet anyone meaningful in my life.'

'I have already wasted numerous opportunities of meeting someone special in my life.'

'I am constantly losing potential opportunities such as new business from sales calls.'

'I have lost a lot of money and will continue to lose a lot of money as I am not reaching my sales targets.'

3. **Arrive at the decision to rid yourself of this fear** – you must make a firm decision to eliminate this fear. You could write down a list of positive statements to support your decision and repeat them to yourself as often as possible.

   For example,

   'I am comfortable with approaching anyone.'

   'I enjoy calling on new clients.'

4. **Start from this moment on to take steps towards ridding yourself of this fear** – as of now, list the action steps required to rid yourself of this fear.

   For example,

   'I will make an effort to be more approachable and friendly every day to all I meet.'

   'I will make an effort to speak to that friendly person in the gym.'

   'I will make an extra 10 new business calls every day starting from today.'

5. **End result of expelling your fear** – the end result is the rewards or advantages you stand to gain from ridding yourself of this fear. Write a list of these advantages and place it where you can see it every day. This will motivate and drive you to 'erase' this fear.

   For example,

   'I have met a wonderful and caring person, with whom I plan to spend the rest of my life.'

   'My salary has now trebled, as I have numerous new clients.'

Choose to live your life to its fullest without fear

It is never too late to address your fears. You must realise that most of your fears come and go so rapidly and the majority of them never materialise. So don't join the countless people who live unfulfilled lives because they avoided doing what they really wanted for fear of the consequences.

We must try to rediscover the child within us and create a healthy appetite for life and the challenges it has to offer. Fear can only limit our lives and make us cringe at challenges and the unknown.

Choose to live your life to its fullest without fear.

Chapter 10

Can you beat depression?

'You are not, what you think you are; what you think, you are.'
Norman Vincent Peale

Ever had those days when you're feeling down in the dumps; when you don't have the will or energy to get up in the morning; when everything around you looks bleak and grey; when you picture your future only filled with doom and gloom and you're asking: 'Why me?' 'What's the use of going on?' 'Why bother?' 'No one understands and no one cares.' Chances are you're feeling depressed!

Never underestimate the destructive power of depression. It is an immensely forceful and often overpowering state of mind, that can reek havoc if left uncontrolled and has been known to result in tragedy, even death.

Can depression be controlled?

Depression is not like a disease that can be spread or a virus that you can catch. It doesn't just appear out of nowhere like a ghost in the dark and spring upon you without warning. Believe it or not, **you make it happen!** You create your own depression as well as all the other results in your life, through the thoughts you dwell upon, your behaviour and the actions you take. There is no other way!

We are not saying that it is wrong to be depressed. We all get depressed at some stage in our lives. Sometimes, for reasons beyond our control. What we want you to understand, is that if you can create the state of depression through your thoughts, behaviour and actions, then you too can change and control it through the right thoughts, behaviour and actions.

The problem with most people, when it comes to changing and controlling their mental states, is that they have this unyielding and totally misguided idea that they cannot control anything that happens in their mind. We have gone to great lengths in previous chapters to prove otherwise and can truthfully say that you can control your mind through your thoughts. So you can control the subsequent behaviour and actions you take, resulting in your mental state. In other words you can control how you feel – happy or depressed, excited or bored, relaxed or tense.

Think depressed; be depressed!

Remember that you are what you think and ultimately your thoughts will make up your life. If you think miserable thoughts, you will be miserable. If you think exciting and motivating thoughts you will be enthusiastic and motivated. So if you think depressing thoughts, you will be depressed. What you think is of vital importance to ascertain not only who you are, but also how you are.

Whether you lose money at the races, drive into your neighbour's Mercedes, fail an exam, get dumped by a loved one or your house burns down, remember that it is not these things that make you depressed; it is how or what you think about them that makes you depressed. In other words it is how you interpret the situation.

As mentioned before, you have indirectly contributed to everything that has happened and will still happen in your life, whether good or bad. Every decision and action you have taken; every thought and feeling you have had – has resulted in your life as it is today. It is a fact that negative thoughts will attract negative experiences in your life.

Thoughts like, 'I hate life.' 'I can't do it.' 'It always happens to me', cloud your memory. So even when something good does come along, you involuntarily drive it away by saying things like, 'it can't possibly last'.

Also dwelling on negative memories from the past will create negative feelings and promote further negative experiences. All this negativity spells depression. Dwell on negatives and you will without a doubt attract the powerful emotional state of depression.

Join the pessimists and you're sure to join the depressed, for they seem to go hand in hand. It's a vicious circle where people are pessimistic because they're depressed and depressed because they're pessimistic. It's up to you to break out of your depression and to avoid being trapped in this negative behaviour pattern.

Many depressed people, when trying to escape this state, make the grave mistake of trying to drown their sorrows in alcohol or experiment with drugs that transport them into a temporary world where, 'all is well, happy and thrilling'. Or there are those who try and eat themselves out of depression, bingeing and gorging themselves on anything they can lay their hands on. The sad thing is that the depression has not gone anywhere. It's still there, waiting patiently for the drug abusers to return from their 'trip', the drinkers to awaken from their drunken stupor and the eaters to finish their last morsel. Then it returns, usually more intense than ever. The degree of their depression is sure to have increased dramatically.

Learn and take action

There are countless stories of people that succeeded in life, only because some tragic event or major downfall caused them to take positive action and change for the better. They learnt from their experiences, putting it behind them and concentrated rather on the endless possibilities of the future.

So unless you suffer from a chemical imbalance in your brain that has to be treated medically, you can help yourself beat depression. Nobody in their right mind wants to remain depressed indefinitely.

The key to breaking out from the hold of depression is 'action'. You must take action either to avoid it or to get rid of it once it is there.

Chapter 11

Avoiding depression!

*'Two men looked out from prison bars,
One saw the mud, the other saw the stars.'*

Dale Carnegie.

When things go wrong and you feel that life has handed you a rotten deal, what do you do? Do you do what most of us do, throwing in the towel and saying, 'I can't handle this. Why me? I give up.'

Or do you do the complete opposite, making the best of your situation and succeeding even with the odds stacked against you? You ask yourself, 'What can I learn from this unfavourable event? How can I better my present situation?'

Succeeding with the odds stacked against you

Life handed Dale Berman a rotten deal, yet she succeeded even with the odds stacked against her. It would have been so easy to say 'Why me, I quit!' and wallow in self-pity. But no, she certainly made the best of her situation.

Dale has fought off cancer for the past 12 years. She was diagnosed in 1985 as having breast cancer. Both breasts had to be removed. The cancer returned some years later and radiotherapy was the answer that time.

It then showed its ugly face again in the form of lumps under her arm, which were cut out. After a long remission when she thought she had at last beaten cancer, it returned in October 1997. This time more vicious than ever before in the form of full-blown lung cancer.

Dale refused to give up her fight and never once dwelled on self- pity. In all the time she fought off cancer, she did not blame others or circumstances for her condition. Instead she was always jovial, positive and determined to win.

We spoke to her whilst she was undergoing chemotherapy to treat her lung cancer. She came across so optimistic and positive.

She said, ' The mind is a wonderful thing, because when your body is going crazy, it says to you, that giving in is out of the question and this can be beaten.' Dale continued, 'You learn to live life one day at a time, appreciating every moment and never taking for granted what you have.'

She has retained her sanity and never feels sorry for herself. Her strength, courage and love will always amaze us. This is her fourth time around with the 'BIG BAD WOLF' and she still will not let him blow the house down. It is definitely mind over matter. Her mind will simply not allow her body to give in and through optimism and a sense of self worth she has fought the cancer with all her might. Medicines can help, but the patient's attitude is also extremely important, particularly with life threatening diseases.

Five months after her diagnosis, Dale was re-tested and doctors were amazed to find no trace of cancer.

The impact self-communication has on your health

The problem with diseases such as cancer, aids, multiple sclerosis and other serious, debilitating ailments, is that they all have very negative, destructive and limiting beliefs associated with them. People have read about them, heard of the negative experiences of others, seen television reports and watched movies about the suffering and trauma of the victims.

Thus it is no wonder that a patient diagnosed with cancer often immediately panics, with a feeling of helplessness and future doom. Often depression sets in as they feel they have nothing to look forward to anymore, only suffering and death. It has even been found that labelling a patient with one of these diseases, actually has a negative effect on their immune system, thereby worsening their condition.

These people are looking at the worst case-scenario. Rather than envisaging death, see life, health and hope. Where there is hope, there is always a chance. Believe that there is a possibility of pulling through and it becomes so much more real. Believe in yourself, your health and your bodies' capability to overcome all. Envisage the healing process. See your body healing itself and help build up your immune system through optimism, positive thinking and a feeling of self worth. (We explore the powerful technique of visualisation more closely in Part 4)

Medical researchers have recognised that your health is influenced to a great extent by the way you communicate with yourself. It has been proved without a doubt that the depth to which any illness affects you, depends largely upon what you repeatedly tell yourself about your life and who you are. So, if you feel great about yourself and the life you have, you will be far healthier than if you feel unhappy about life in general. It is a fact that numerous serious conditions have responded unbelievably well to the simple act of positive self-communication.

Three reasons why you should try

When you are feeling depressed and it seems like there is nothing you can do to make things better; here are three reasons why you should try. After all you have nothing to lose!

One: You may succeed by turning the situation around in your favour.

Two: Even if you don't succeed; in trying you have changed your frame of mind from negative to positive by focusing on the solution rather than the problem. This positive state will steer you away from depression.

Three: Even if you don't succeed; in trying you may have taken positive action, which could result in new and exciting opportunities showing themselves.

Utilise the healing power of the mind

We recommend that you try this short little exercise daily, to help protect you from the gloom and doom of depression as well as any other ailment that plagues you. One cannot underestimate the extraordinary healing power of this exercise and there have been many documented reports proving that this and similar exercises have helped cure a number of ailments including depression.

By doing this exercise for a few minutes each day, you will be surprised at how invigorated you will feel for the rest of the day. It should make you feel healthy, strong and good about yourself, thus warding off depression and illness.

All you need to do is to find a quiet spot where you can relax and close your eyes for a few minutes. We know it will sound a little crazy, but it does work if you allow your imagination to explore the concept of self-healing. It is a fact that your mind has the power to heal your body and itself.

All you need to do now is picture your body as the complex machinery it is. Truly believe that it can heal itself of anything. Actually picture your body cleansing and healing itself by thinking of crystal clear mountain water flushing throughout your body, washing out all impurities. See your blood flowing smoothly and your heart pumping with ease. Think of your body as healthy, satisfied and strong. Picture all the good in your body fighting, destroying and driving out the bad.

Let these thoughts of health and vitality flow through your body, filling your bloodstream, organs, tissues and every cell you possess. Think of it as though you were gulping down a powerful health shake, filled to the brim with goodness that flows to every part of you, spreading its energy and strengthening everything it touches.

How to keep depression from your door

Here is another short exercise to make you feel great about yourself and keep depression from your door.

All we want you to do is write a long list of your good points. Try and include more than 15 points, listing anything you can possibly come up with and covering every aspect of your life. Forget modesty, as no one has to see it but you – so get going by putting pen to paper and listing your strong points. For example:

'I am a good friend.'
'I am a good painter.'
'I am trustworthy.'
'I am good with people.'
'I've got a loving family'
'I'm a good gardener'
'I make people laugh'
'I'm good at my job'
'I'm ambitious'
'I can scuba dive'

Now keep this list close at hand – perhaps in a personal file, in your diary or in a top drawer where you can retrieve it easily for those days you need a lift.

So when you're feeling down in the dumps and useless, with depression rearing its ugly head, you can squash it by looking over the numerous reasons you have to feel great and proud of yourself. By reminding yourself of your positive traits, you create the necessary positive energy to steer you in the right direction.

Avoid depression by adopting a Positive Mental Attitude

One of the easiest ways to avoid depression is to distance yourself from all negatives and to promote only positives. This means shutting out those that put you down and rob you of your good feelings. It also means closing the door on those negative people whose influence so easily rubs off on you. Don't let anyone take away your good feelings and lust for life!

At the same time push aside anything – memories, thoughts and experiences that could eat away at your good feelings about yourself and life in general. Instead, make a point of always surrounding yourself with positive people, thinking only positive thoughts, remembering only positive memories and focusing on where you want to go in life.

Yes, we all have our down times, when our good feelings are eroded by circumstances and events, but we can avoid falling headlong into depression by adopting a Positive Mental Attitude.

Chapter 12

How to drive out negative mental states

*'When you're down and Life is a frown
Don't despair for a solution is there.'*
Warren Veenman & Sally Eichhorst

Focus on the irreplaceable assets you have

We mentioned earlier that an effective way to avoid depression would be to focus on your strong points. In the same way you can also wipe out depression and put a smile on your face by focusing on the irreplaceable assets you have that money just can't buy. Stop for a minute and think about all the assets and riches you possess - your health, your eyes, your ears, your limbs, your loved ones and anything else to which you simply cannot pin a price tag.

Would you sell both your hands and feet for a winning lottery ticket? What about your eyes? Your arms? Your legs? Your children? What are they worth to you? Surely you wouldn't sell any of these things for all the money in the world?

Sadly, most of us never stop to give these things even a second thought.

Instead we tend to focus always on what we don't have, which leads to misery and depression.

Think of those far worse off than you

Another excellent remedy to combat depression is to think of those far worse off than you. When we are depressed, it is difficult to think of others, as we tend to have a selfish outlook. Our problems become all encompassing and we don't care much about anything else. However we must tear ourselves away from our problem for a moment and consider those who have already or are presently enduring worse.

There have been countless people who faced excessive emotional and or physical hardship and traumas and somehow found the courage to overcome these things. We should compare some of our minor problems that throw us into bouts of self-pity and depression to that of these courageous people who have overcome or achieved the unthinkable. We would soon have to sheepishly admit that we don't really have a serious enough situation to warrant a full- blown 'woe is me' session. We would also realise that if there are others who were able to overcome far worse than we have ever encountered, then what is stopping us from resolving or overcoming our situation?

Just think of how many people would do anything to trade places with you right now – people who would welcome your problems compared to theirs!

What about people suffering from a 'terminal illness' or a seriously debilitating disease. Are they not far worse off than most of us?

These people have two choices, they can either choose to succumb to depression or they can choose to muster up all their energies to fight their disease. Through sheer belief in themselves, courage, determination and an altogether positive mental attitude, they may even overcome it. Even if they don't, they have given it their all and are a beacon of courage and encouragement for those who suffer the same fate.

Sandy Potgieter was such a person.

It all started late October 1992 with a visit to the Dentist and then a referral to a Periodontist to cure a simple abscess. Dozens of injections later, Sandy Potgieter went into convulsions as a major nerve was hit. Little did she know that this would be the least of her worries and only the beginning of her traumatic journey.

The following day Sandy awoke to a violent headache, which progressively worsened. She was hospitalised and diagnosed with meningitis. Two days later she could not move from the waist down as paralysis set in. Six weeks later, doctors told her that the damage was irreparable and she would be paralysed for life. Sandy learned to accept her fate and cope with life as a paraplegic. In her wheelchair she felt she could still manoeuvre herself and make herself useful.

This was short-lived as seven months later a violent and worse headache again struck. Sandy awoke the following morning to find she was paralysed from the neck down except for partial use of her arms. They operated on the top of her spine with little effect. She had to learn all sorts of things again, including feeding herself.

With her third attack, Sandy was eventually diagnosed as having multiple sclerosis, possibly triggered off by the meningitis. Sandy did not however allow herself to be depressed. Her husband and family willed her not to give up. She had always been a fighter and fight she would.

Another major attack came and she lost complete use of her arms as well as becoming paralysed on the one side of her face. She couldn't swallow or talk and everyone felt it was over. 'Tickets', as she would say with her positively contagious sense of humour.

She attended speech therapy where she learnt to talk again on a breath of air. Through putting a spoon on her tongue they also taught her to swallow again.

" I very seldom feel really down, ' Sandy said. 'I don't want sympathy or even to talk about it. Not that I want to block it out, I just want to get on with things. I accept it and live one day at a time."

With her next attack she lost her eyesight completely. First it was blurry, then darkness came. She recalled waking in the morning and asking her husband, John, to please open the curtains, but they were open, only she could not see.

Each attack seemed to take a bit more away from her but her philosophy remained that it was no good complaining as it made herself and everyone else around her miserable.

Sandy continued, 'Every day I would peer out and try and see, until one day I did! I have really learned to appreciate what I still have.' She said she wished she could tap into the ninety something percent of her brain she didn't use, as she was sure she would then be able to move freely again.

This was clearly an extremely positive lady. 'Once you come to terms with it, you either give up or fight on' she said. 'I really believe that if you're going to think negative thoughts and complain all the time, it pushes people away. Friends don't want to come and hear about how ill I am. I've got to think positive. I don't like to be treated differently.'

Even though each attack seemed to lead to further deterioration, she said she didn't dwell on what was going to happen in the future. She lived day to day and appreciated every one, knowing she just had to persevere and learn to manage herself.

'Somehow you do cope – you get this inner strength and carry on.' She said many people may think, what's the reason for living if things can't improve? But every attack made her more determined to fight and keep going.

She was grateful for the things she did still have, saying one thing she had really learnt to do was appreciate things she once took for granted. Listening to people complaining, Sandy often wished she could make them realise how silly their complaints were.

She may have lost a few things but she still had a strong will and belief in herself. She still had her wonderful husband and daughters, she still had her sense of humour and felt it was incredibly important to keep one sane and happy no matter what the circumstances. What a wonderful, brave and courageous lady this was!

Sandy passed away in April 1998 and remains a shining light of courage and encouragement to all the lives she touched.

Whenever we are feeling depressed or sorry for ourselves, we take a moment to think about Sandy's five year ordeal. This makes us aware of just how insignificant our worries and problems are. Next time you are feeling depressed, take a moment to think about this yourself!

Identify 'feel good' activities

Remember that depression is an emotional state of mind describing the way you feel. You can beat depression by making yourself feel good. How? By simply identifying activities that make you feel good or happy and then actively indulging in one or more of them to distract you from your depression.

It could be anything like, dancing, listening to music, reading, sketching, exercising and anything else that tickles your fancy. When we're feeling a little flat, we take long walks on the beach and enjoy a cappuccino while watching the sun set and drinking in the fresh sea air. When things really get us down, we found what works best for us, is a good, solid sweat session at the local gym.

There must be at least one positive activity that you really enjoy doing which would certainly be a welcome alternative to feeling miserable and depressed. You can even try out some totally new and exciting experiences. Depending on what you have and have not done, this could include horse riding on the beach, skiing, sky diving, scuba diving, white water rafting, mountain climbing or what ever else 'blows your hair back.'

There are so many wildly outrageous and adventurous possibilities out there, so much for you still to do and see. This is certainly a good way to get your lust for life well oiled again. You will feel the energy racing through your veins as you encounter a wonderfully new experience and feel deliciously alive.

Of course this does not include experimenting with addictive sources like drugs or turning to alcohol as a temporary distraction to make you feel better; these are usually the source of destruction rather than construction.

Every negative has a positive

Janine is a typical example of someone who has managed to look at the positive side of every negative situation and experience she has encountered throughout her life.

If you met Janine, you would never guess that this confident, intelligent, self-motivated and 'totally together' person had been through so much.

Janine comes from an unstable, extremely disruptive and troubled background. Both her parents were problematic. Her mother was a manic depressive and her father suffered from paranoid schizophrenia. They were extremely poor and always battling to make ends meet. At a young age her older brother was involved in a freak accident leaving him paralyzed and mentally disturbed. To top it off her younger brother, whom she was extremely fond of, was killed.

Janine was left in an unsettled environment. She said that all these negatives actually helped her become the independent and confident person she is today. Her negative past made her all the more determined to better herself and her situation.

Janine said, ' I don't blame anybody. Overcoming my background just made me more confident. You come out of it stronger as you know more. Now nothing really phases me anymore as I've been through so much. I learnt a lot of things that maybe take others a lifetime to learn.'

Janine continued, 'Whenever I feel negative, I think about that guy with no legs who moves around town on a skateboard. He's always got a great big smile on his face and seems so cheerful and happy despite his situation. Then I can't help feeling great and positive about my life. I never blame anyone or anything for success or failure in my life. I know it's entirely up to me.'

We can all learn from Janine.

There are many terrible things that most of us will encounter in life. Although we may feel that we have no control whatsoever over them, we must remember that we can control the most important thing – how we will let these things affect our lives.

There can be numerous interpretations of the same 'bad' experience. So what we urge you to do is to identify the most positive interpretation and focus only on that, putting the rest behind you. Learn to look for the positives in every negative situation. By doing this, you will win in life with every lesson learnt and grow as a person.

See problems as challenges and ask yourself what you can learn from them. If it was just smooth sailing all the way and we were never faced with any challenges, we would never utilise our full potential, as we would never have reasons to push ourselves to the limit and test our endurance.

Next time you're feeling depressed for any particular reason, view your situation as one of life's challenges and focus on what you can learn from the situation. Take a closer look at the problem, seeing it in another light and from a different angle. Possibly you will find a better interpretation that will make you feel a lot better.

Secret formula to attract riches and happiness

If we told you that we had a simple formula which would do the following for you:

- **Remove depression, fear and worry from your mind**
- **Create an abundance of happiness**
- **Attract new friends**
- **Receive warmth and affection from all you meet**
- **Create pride in yourself**
- **Produce an aura around you that would attract riches and blessings from others**
- **Allow you to sleep peacefully at night**
- **Create a tremendous boost for your physical and mental wellbeing**

Would you be interested? If we told you that you need no capital and it doesn't matter who you are or what your present situation is; surely we've captured your interest now?

What is this formula that can so easily eradicate depression, attract riches and great happiness and requires no great effort on your part?

To be friendly and helpful to all you meet.

That's it! From this moment on, this is all you need to do every day to attain the above results. Create a desire within you to be friendly and helpful to all you meet. It is important to remember that you must do this without expecting any rewards in return.

How do you know when you have succeeded in helping others and making others happy? Simply, when you have put a smile on another's face.

Of course this doesn't mean you have to follow in the steps of Superman, saving lives left, right and centre, or become a Saint and give everything you own to others. Sometimes it is just the small things in life that make all the difference.

Prove it to yourself. From this moment on, give a friendly greeting to all those you come in contact with regardless of their position in life.

Show genuine interest in those around you. Offer kindness and encouragement to those clearly in need thereof. Compliment and thank from the heart. Offer a helping hand to an old person laden with parcels. Give, no matter how little, to charity. Join a voluntary charity group, where all you need give is a little of your time and effort. The list of ways to help others and put a smile on their faces is endless.

Strangely, life has a way of returning your good deeds and sometime, somehow you will be blessed tenfold – "what goes around, comes around." So the more you give of yourself, the more you will get. Just as, "the more you share, the more you will receive."

How does helping others stop us from being depressed? When you are helping others you are interrupted from brooding about yourself. Instead of focusing on your worries and fears, you concentrate on the positive act of making another happy, thereby creating a positive and healthy state of mind.

Can having a genuine interest in other people really have such a positive impact on you? You bet it can! Warren tried it and it certainly worked wonders for him!

Warren's story

I used the same parking garage, walked the same route to my office and employed the same staff for over 5 years. I never took much notice or showed much interest in the people I passed or came into contact with day in and day out. I'm pretty sure they never really noticed me either.

After reading about the advantages of a similar formula, I decided to try it out. The next morning, as I drove into the parking garage, I blew my hooter and greeted the parking attendant. After an awkward pause of disbelief and surprise, he smiled and enthusiastically returned the greeting. When I parked my car, I walked to the security guard at the exit, asked his name and made a mental note to remember it. I gave a warm and friendly greeting to the chap selling flowers, the newspaperman, the lady at the fruit stall and the security guard at my office building. I walked into my office and greeted all my staff, showing genuine interest in their wellbeing. You should have seen all their expressions of surprise and pleasure!

The next morning when I arrived at the parking garage, I'd made a new friend – the parking attendant. He gave me a big grin when I arrived and he quickly directed me to a prime parking spot that eventually became mine for the duration of my stay there. As I strolled towards my office, you would have thought I was the most popular man around. It seems I had new friends in all sorts of places - the flower seller, the newspaper man, the security guard, the lady at the fruit stall – they all gave me the biggest smiles and greetings as though I were a long lost friend. From that day on, they couldn't do enough for me. If I needed fruit, I always got the best and a little extra. I even got free flowers for my 'other half' on a regular basis. My relationship with my staff improved dramatically, resulting in my business flourishing all the more.

Overall, by adopting this formula, it not only put me in an extremely happy and positive state of mind every day, but I received all the benefits mentioned above.

So if you want to achieve these benefits, we recommend that you start now. From this moment on, everyone you meet, whether it's the chap at the corner who polishes your shoes, the security guard at the door, the lift operator, your secretary, your spouse, your children and every living person you meet, give a smile, talk, listen, understand, care for and give a kind word to all these people.

Adopt this formula and you are sure to grow from strength to strength, squashing and removing all negative and depressing thoughts. If you keep to yourself and give nothing, you are bound to drown in your own worries, fears and depression.

Learn to laugh more often

When you learn to laugh often, you have discovered one of the greatest treatments for depression. There have been extensive studies into the use of laughter and humour to combat illness, including the mental state of depression. There have even been documented reports of people who have been cured with the help of laughter. Recent research has conclusively found that the act of laughing causes two vital kinds of hormones, encephalins and endorphins, to be discharged into the brain, relieving not only depression, but also pain and tension.

It is a well-known fact that people suffering from depression are far more prone to illness than happy people who laugh often. Certain hospitals even have so called 'humour rooms' filled with all sorts of things to make patients laugh – cartoons, comedies and humorous magazines.

Anyone can develop the art of laughing. Haven't you noticed how those who laugh easily are less prone to depression and seem to be far more socially accepted?

So why not practise the art of looking on the bright side of every situation and developing a wonderful sense of humour? It's natural; it costs you nothing and it's such fun! Learn to laugh as often as you can so it becomes a habit. In this way you're sure to have more fun and enjoy life more. You will certainly be a lot happier, attracting others to you and seeing a dramatic improvement in every aspect of your life.

Take charge of your life

Sadly, there are many people who never quite find happiness, instead repelling it. They tend to hang onto traumas and tragedies for as long as possible, dragging out their misery for years.

These people are only punishing themselves more by refusing to let go of the past. It's a shame! You only have one life so why waste so much of it being depressed? You have to learn to let go of the past and get on with the act of living your life to its fullest. Go through that old closet that is your mind and do some spring-cleaning. Throw out all those burdensome bad memories and experiences you've been hoarding. Rather make room for better memories and experiences still to come in the future.

Whatever your current problems are, you must realise that it's not the end of the world. There is still so much for you to live for, things to do, places to see and people to meet. Your time here is short; so why not choose to make the best of it?

We all fall at some stage, some harder than others. But much like falling off a horse, one has to immediately climb back on that saddle and take charge before confidence is lost and fear sets in. Likewise, after any knock in life we must immediately fight back and try again before depression sets in and self-esteem is lost.

Chapter 13

Secret to happiness

If you want to be happy for life, love what you do
love who you are
and love who you're with!
Warren Veenman & Sally Eichhorst

It's your choice...

Happiness, that 'elusive thing' we're all after, which somehow manages to slip from the grasp of most, escaping them at every attempt of capture. There are those who travel to all corners of the earth in the hope of finding it. There are those who buy bigger houses, cars and toys to capture it. There are those who drink more and party harder to feel it even for a fleeting moment. There are those who revolve their world around a lover, spouse or another, relying solely on them to supply the happiness they crave.

Then there are countless people who believe in the theory of 'happiness comes later, when I have done this or that, or when I have overcome this or that.' It is no wonder then, that happiness eludes most, as people are searching for it in the wrong places and for the wrong reasons, setting all sorts of prerequisites for its existence. Well, it cannot be found or simply appear from nowhere and it certainly does not just happen to you.

The secret to happiness is knowing what you want from your life and why you want it. Happiness is something very personal, that each and every one of us is capable of. Happiness is not a matter of luck, possessions, ability, money, fame or glory. It is not up to someone or some event to come along and make you happy. It's all up to you! You don't have to wait for anything to make you happy. **You can be happy right now by making a firm decision to choose to be happy.**

Promote feeling good

Feeling good, leads to a happier you, so why not work on making yourself feel good more often. It seems crazy, but it is a fact that most of us have countless ways of making ourselves feel bad, compared with our pathetic attempts to promote feeling good. We would be a great deal happier if we worked at minimising the numerous ways that we have developed to feel miserable. We should rather concentrate on building and strengthening our attempts to feel happy. By doing this, we would make it very easy on ourselves to feel happy, whilst making it very difficult to feel depressed.

Just as you work at creating your own depression, you too can work at creating or manufacturing your own happiness. No one wants to remain miserable, bitter, sad and depressed indefinitely, but everyone wants exactly the opposite – to be happy indefinitely.

Find reasons why you should be happy right now!

Make a firm mental decision to be happy right now. To support your decision, you should think of all the reasons why you should be happy right now. Write them down and add to your list whenever you come up with a new reason.

Some of your reasons could include:
'I am happy because I am healthy, fit and able.'
'I am happy because I have a roof over my head and food in my stomach.'

'I am happy because I am loved.'

When things go wrong and you feel you are carrying the world on your shoulders. When everything seems to be falling apart around you, revert your attention to your list of reasons of why you should be happy right now.

Read your list as often as possible, every morning, day and night. Really work at convincing yourself that you are happy and you will be. Think only happy thoughts and you will attract only happy experiences and manufacture a happy and healthy state of mind. Do this often enough and it will soon become second nature; you will naturally be happy. You will have succeeded at something many geniuses, heroes, famous stars and millionaires have failed at.

> *'There are two things to aim at in life:*
> *First, to get what you want; and, after that, to enjoy it.*
> *Only the wisest of mankind achieve the second.'*
> **Logan Pearsall Smith.**

There was never a more true and wiser word spoken. So many people have reached the pinnacle of success by becoming top runners in their chosen professions. They had a dream to succeed like you and I. Many of them surpassed even their own expectations.

Why then have so many of these people turned to alcohol, drugs, depression and sometimes even to suicide? Yes, they may be successful, but happiness has still eluded them and they often don't know how to make themselves truly happy. So they turn to drugs or alcohol to do the job for them. Or they remain bitter and depressed, unable to truly enjoy their success.

Money and fame does not guarantee happiness

A prime example is the music industry, notorious for drug overdoses and suicides amongst those stars often at the peak of their careers. The death of Michael Hutchence, lead singer and main lyricist with INXS for the past 20 years, paints a sad and all too familiar picture.

Unfortunately Hutchence's name can be added to the long and growing list of rock legends, who took their own lives at the height of their careers. Jimi Hendrix, the legendary guitarist, took an overdose. Jim Morrison of the Doors was found dead in a bath and was a known drug abuser. Kurt Cobain, lead singer of Nirvana, shot himself. Janis Joplin died of an overdose. Brian Jones, of the Rolling Stones was found dead in his swimming pool. It even stretches as far back as Elvis Presley whose drug abuse claimed even the King of Rock himself.

These people all died whilst at the top, still young, with so much time left and so much still to live for. Why then, when they had fame, glory, wealth and everything they could imagine, were they responsible for their own demise?

Why would someone who seems to have everything, want to end their lives or turn to destructive sources like drugs which eventually becomes uncontrollable and destroys them? In fact, why do so many of us who should be happy, never enjoy happiness.

Why does happiness elude us?

♦ **Maybe those who ended their lives felt they no longer had anything to live for?**

They had reached their peak and loved it there. Possibly they feared the future – maybe they felt that things could not possibly get better, only worse. This could lead to a paralysing fear of losing their fame and popularity. Perhaps they could not live with the thought that one day they may be old news – rather die whilst at the top and be remembered that way. Their happiness relied on remaining at the top, to be adored by millions of 'fans'. Take that away and they were robbed of their happiness.

This is a typical picture of those who base their happiness on something they cannot completely control. These people could not control the level of their popularity and fame forever.

If our happiness is based on something or someone we cannot control, we are destined for unhappiness. Another example is someone who falls into a deep depression or even goes as far as committing suicide over a lost love. They base all their happiness on that one person and when that person is gone, happiness leaves with them and they can only envisage a life of eternal sadness without their lost soul mate. Nothing and no one should have this power over you.

♦ **Perhaps these people reached their goals and realised their dreams, only to find that they were still not happy.**

It seemed to everyone else and even to them that they had everything their hearts desired and yet they knew that happiness had still eluded them.

Possibly they felt that they were incapable of ever being truly happy. This depressing thought could lead to alcohol and drug abuse as an alternative source to achieve happiness and ultimately to their sad and untimely death. It seems that these people eventually did not know how to make themselves feel good or happy without the use of drugs and alcohol.

Happiness is a state of mind. It is not something that occurs naturally with the accumulation of wealth and fame. Many make the mistake of associating happiness with money, power and glory. Acquiring any one or more of these may not lead directly to happiness. You must be happy within yourself.

Forget your status and what you have. Look at who you really are and what you really want from life. Then think about what makes you feel good and what will make you happy in life. Don't wait for fame to knock on your door or wealth to fall into your lap before you are happy. You can be happy without them and you will find that your happy and cheerful disposition will help you to achieve your goals more easily.

If your goals are fame and wealth – remember, don't rely only on them for your happiness; rely on yourself.

♦ **Perhaps those who were successful and never truly achieved happiness were too hard on themselves.**

Maybe they had a set of standards, which they could not abide by or live up to and therefore they would not allow themselves the luxury of happiness.

There are many people who are far too hard on themselves, laying down certain rules to be met before they allow happiness into their lives. This only serves to add unnecessary stress and pressure to life's challenges. To ensure long term happiness, you must allow yourself the luxury of feeling happy as often as possible and whenever you want. There is nothing wrong with rules and standards to guide you through life, but they must not be allowed to deter your happiness. Choose to be happy now and your journey through life is sure to be a lot more fun and a great deal more fruitful.

Choose happiness!

We all desire never-ending happiness, yet it is only a handful who achieve it. If you wish to join that handful, you must firstly have a clear idea of what you want from life. You must also realise that happiness is not something you look for and find. It is something that you must create!

Forget about relying on something or someone for your happiness. For true, long lasting happiness you can rely only on yourself. Never put off being happy; rather choose to be happy now and fill your mind with your reasons for happiness. Do the things that make you feel good. Learn to see the bright side of life and fill your world with laughter. Remember, 'He who laughs, lasts!' Devote some time and energy to making others happy and it will return to you tenfold.

The happiness that eludes most of us, is in fact well within everyone's grasp, if only they choose to create it and attract it.

Part 4

The Road to Attaining Your Dreams

I sit in a boat, on a stagnant sea.
Going neither here nor there.
I have come to the realisation that I'm going nowhere,
For I have no goals.
Warren Veenman & Sally Eichhorst

Chapter 14

Why Goals?

'A man's reach should exceed his grasp, else what's a heaven for?'
Robert Browning

How many of us plan our weekends and annual leave down to the finest detail? To plan our holiday we would make inquiries about destinations and accommodation. We would phone and make the bookings, obtain brochures and make a day to day plan of sights to see and things to do. Sadly we go into little or no detail when it comes to planning our lives. Most of us even plan our deaths in great detail in the form of a will, yet make little or no effort to plan our living years.

Most of us have many dreams and wishes about what we would like to be or have in life. But for most of us, these remain only dreams and wishes, never to be fulfilled.

Why do so many of us never reach our dreams?

Possibly because we never quite know what we want and where we are going in life. Or if we do know what we want, we don't really believe in our capability to achieve it. So we fumble along aimlessly in one direction and then suddenly decide to change course, as the grass may be greener on the other side. We attempt one thing and at the first sign of an obstacle, we drop it for another. We allow ourselves to stagnate and convince ourselves that we don't have what it takes to reach our dreams.

Shooting at targets whilst blindfolded!

The end result is that we never quite get anywhere and seem to be continually in a cloud of bewilderment, never really knowing what we want. It's as though we're putting together a jigsaw puzzle without knowing what the final picture looks like.

What we lack is definite goals. Unless we have a crystal-clear idea of what we want from life, there is no way we will accomplish our dreams.

The importance of setting goals can be illustrated by a study undertaken some time back, whereby a number of graduates of a prestigious University were interviewed about goal setting. It was found that only three percent of those interviewed had written goals.

Twenty years later, the same graduates were re-interviewed regarding their progress in life. It was concluded that the three percent who had set goals, were abundantly more successful than the rest of the class in every respect. Thus the importance of goals cannot be underestimated.

If you are still not convinced about the importance of goals, why don't you search for your high school annual or class photograph. You will find that many of your classmates shared similarities such as education, age and economic opportunities. Yet if you had to look at them today, you would probably find that some are battling to make ends meet, others are living a life of mediocrity and then there are those few who have achieved great things; whether it be wealth, fame, power or happiness.

If you all started off on a fairly equal footing, why did some fail and some succeed? Was it luck? Were they more talented or gifted? Did opportunities fall into their laps? We doubt that very much! More often than not, those who achieved their dreams had a set of goals and therefore knew precisely where they were going and took the necessary action to get there.

To ensure success in life, we must learn to set goals. So many of us realise too late and wake up to find that life has passed us by. We feel the cold chilly wind of an empty and fruitless past and wish we had done so much more with our lives. **Don't become one of these people!**

Effective goal setting can be compared to the work of an artist. As with an artist who has a multitude of colours available to him, you have a multitude of opportunities and capabilities available to you. It is entirely up to the artist whether or not he paints a bright, lively masterpiece or a dull, lifeless and average picture. In the same respect, it is up to you whether or not you use all the opportunities and capabilities available to you to build a bright and successful life. You can only do this through effective goal setting.

How do you practice effective goal setting?

The following 6 chapters cover a highly effective 6-point goal setting program that we have devised to help you achieve anything you have ever dreamed of.

Chapter 15

Step 1 — How to attain your dreams

What do you really want?

'We are what and where we are because we have first imagined it.'
Donald Curtis

The many success stories we have researched and the multitude of people we have spoken to from all walks of life who managed to attain their goals, had one thing in common. They each had a distinct picture in their minds of what they wanted from life. It is our sincere belief that ninety nine percent of people are disillusioned with their lives because they have no clear idea in their minds of the type of life they want to lead.

If you are not making the headway you would like to make in relation to your capabilities, it is obvious that you do not have a clear idea of what you want from life. In other words, it is simply because you either do not have goals or if you do, they are not precise enough. In order to live the life of your dreams, you must have a distinct picture of exactly what you want.

Before proceeding, we would like to emphasise that you should not simply read this chapter as you would a normal book. Rather, get actively involved, by taking part in the following two action steps. If you don't, you will certainly not obtain the maximum benefit this book has to offer.

Action step1

Find a quiet relaxing spot, with paper and pen at hand. It could be anywhere in your home – from the comfort of your bedroom to a corner table with a peaceful view. Here you can take the time to discover what you really and truly want out of life. We again recommend that you do not read past this chapter until you have done this.

We want you to open the door of your imagination as wide as you possibly can and dream of all you have ever wanted in your life. We recommend that you permit yourself to write down anything you wish for, no matter how unlikely it may seem at this stage.

It may be something you would like to become, material possessions you would like to have, a place you would like to travel to, or a person you would like to meet. Whatever it is, write it down.

Remember, at this stage, not to focus on what is possible and what is not. Knowing what you want is the first step to reaching it. So take your time and feel the excitement mounting at the thought of what you want. Write your list now!

Remember there are no limitations except those that you set for yourself. Do not limit your life by disallowing yourself to imagine great possibilities, for fear that you may not be capable of achieving them. Obviously common sense and reason are necessary to a certain degree. If you are a male and would like to give birth to twins, you are definitely throwing common sense out the window! On the other hand, the human mind has produced wonders such as the possibility of space travel and numerous other once unbelievable and laughable innovations. When we look at technology today, it is obvious that our minds are capable of accomplishing almost anything. So keep your mind open to all possibilities.

Rather think big as it will inspire and therefore move you to action as opposed to thinking small which lacks challenge and excitement.

Action step 2

Now that you have completed your list of dreams and desires, keep the flames of your imagination burning and write about your perfect day. It must be a day in the future when you have achieved all the dreams and desires expressed in Action Step 1.

From the moment you open your eyes in the morning until the moment you close them in the evening - Where will you be? Who will you be with? How will you feel? What will you be doing all day and all evening? What will your home look like and what car will you be driving? Go into detail describing your perfect day; really feel and live it as though you are already there. Capture it all on paper.

Maybe your ideal day would involve enjoying a cocktail with the love of your life, on the balcony of your beautiful home, overlooking the ocean. Let your imagination run wild and envisage the happiest day imaginable, where all your dreams have come true.

You must have an idea of both your perfect day and surroundings, so that you have a clear and precise idea of what you are working towards. If you walk into a shop without knowing what you want beforehand, you'll most likely leave with nothing or perhaps with something you may not really need, thereby wasting your time and money. Likewise, if you approach life with no idea of what you really want, what are your chances of ever living your ideal day? We wrote down our perfect day, and we are now living it. You can too!

Review your life!

In helping people arrive at a clear idea of what they really want from their lives, we ask them this; ' If you were ninety years of age and were reviewing your life, what would you like to see? What would you have accomplished? Where would you have travelled? What would you have now to show for all your years? Are you content and happy with the life you have had up to now?'

If you are unsure about what you really want from your life, we recommend that you envisage yourself as a ninety-year old and ask yourself these same questions.

Now, if you have not already done so, we again challenge you to write down what you want from life and thereby set yourself on the road to achieving your dreams. Surely by now you must have realised the importance of having goals and writing them down in a clear and precise manner. **Do it before going on to the next chapter.**

Create a burning desire to

reach your dreams

If our reasons are strong enough,
We can do almost anything we put our minds to.
Warren Veenman & Sally Eichhorst

You may now be aware of what you want to achieve, but at this stage it may only be something you need, wish, expect or long for. This is of little benefit and is not enough to move you along the path towards success. What you need is to create a burning desire to excite and inspire you to accomplish your goals.

Just as the fuel of a rocket propels it skywards, desire is the fuel that propels us in the direction of our worthwhile goals. Just as you can think of a tall glass of fresh juice on a hot day and feel extremely thirsty, you can stimulate and arouse the feeling of desire by concentrating your thoughts on the rewards you stand to gain upon achievement of your goals.

When you desire something so intensely that you give your all to have it, you will succeed, crushing all obstacles along the way. It is this intense and obsessive desire that makes the difference, separating the winners from the losers.

Desire is the starting point of all achievement.
" Whatever the mind of man can conceive and believe it can achieve."
Napoleon Hill.

If you are to accomplish your dreams and goals you must develop a burning desire, or else, no matter how worthy your goals, you will not achieve them. Often the vital difference between winners and those who come a close second is not so much a variation in ability, approach or method but rather a stronger desire to win.

Gail Deurs had such a desire. Imagine losing sight in one eye and suffering from uncontrollable shaking. Then undergoing radiation treatment and enduring horrendous side effects, causing minute holes all over one's skin as well as feet so swollen that walking becomes unbearable and impossible. Now, imagine doctors being close to amputating both feet. Imagine this same person eighteen months later winning the 100m Gold medal at the 1992 Olympics. Unbelievable? No, Gail Deurs did it! Nothing could stop her. She knew precisely what she wanted and her burning desire to achieve it let nothing stand in her way.

Creating desire

You are now aware that having desire is critically important in reaching your goals. So how do you create it?

You create it by analysing the personal rewards or benefits you stand to gain from achieving your goals.

That's it! There is only this one way to achieve the burning desire so necessary to accomplishing your goals and that is to have worthwhile rewards.

Do this right now. Look at your list of goals (what you want from life) which you completed in Step 1. Now ask yourself the following question and write the answers under each of your written goals:

'What will the benefits and advantages be once I have achieved this goal?'

It is important to write the answers down in the present tense. In other words as though you have already accomplished your goal.

If for example you are overweight and you want to lose 20kg, your list could look like this:
'I feel healthier and more energetic.'
'I feel comfortable in that new costume I only admired on others.'
'I am now a lot more confident and happier with my appearance.'

If your goal is to be extremely wealthy, your list could look like this:
'I now own the home of my dreams overlooking the ocean.'
'I am able to help friends and family who find themselves in financial difficulties.'
'I can now travel to all the places I once only dreamed of visiting.'

This is possibly the only way you can stimulate your desire. You must have a benefit to achieve, or a loss to be avoided. Everything you do in life is for a reason, otherwise why do it? So if you have numerous reasons to do something, you will be far more motivated to do it.

If you cannot list any personal rewards, you have not stated your goal correctly and it is not a goal. If you can find enough reasons why you want to achieve something, you will create the desire that will motivate and drive you to accomplish anything.

Desire stimulates the emotions, making our goals seem real. It is a quality that everyone can develop at no cost. It is a powerful quality that has seen the underprivileged lifted to the ranks of the privileged as well as helping those that should have died beat the odds and live to a ripe old age.

Our desire gives us reasons to forge ahead and make our goals real. It will also drive us towards the creation of a good, solid plan to achieve our goals. Remember that if our reasons are strong enough we can do almost anything we put our minds to. How we do it will seem to naturally follow.

Chapter 17

Step 3 — How to attain your dreams

The Plan

'Saying is one thing and doing is another.'
Montaigne, 'Essays'

Now that you have written down your goals clearly and created a burning desire to achieve them, it is time to devise a plan that will lead you to the fulfilment of your goals. Your written plan must be so distinctly laid out, that there must be no room for confusion or distraction. It must guide you, one step at a time towards the realisation of your goals, lifting them out of the realm of daydreams and onto the road of accomplishment.

If you take a closer look at people who have made a success of their lives, you will notice that the vast majority of them do not have some remarkable gift, distinguishing them from you and I. The difference lies in their ability to take effective action and make things happen for themselves.

If all we needed were dreams to attain our goals, we would all be living our ultimate lives now. Acting on our dreams is what yields results and without positive action, they will remain forever in our imaginations.

A written plan is essential for the attainment of our dreams. It can be likened to the road signs that guide us along the journey to our destination. Written plans, like road signs, will keep us on the right road to our final objective. They will show us the easiest route to get there. They will let us know how far we have travelled and how much further we have to go. They also warn and prepare us for possible danger ahead.

Written plans also help us to master those destroyers of success – procrastination, depression, loss of direction and unnecessary fear and worry. A written plan helps us to organise our life and make better use of the time needed to reach our ideal life.

Although there are those among us who seem to know what they want and have created the necessary desire to achieve it, when it comes to developing a plan of action, they feel it is too difficult and foreboding a task. They therefore come to a grinding halt and never reach their dreams.

In actual fact, developing a plan of action is a relatively simple process that anyone can follow and master.

PLAN OF ACTION

So far you have listed all your dreams (goals) and next to each you have written the personal rewards you will attain upon achieving each goal (to create a burning desire).

Now go back to this list and carefully scan through it, prioritising your goals from most important to least important. Start applying our 5 step action plan below to your most important goal.

Do we have the audacity to tell you that by successfully completing these 5 important tasks you will accomplish your dreams and desires? Yes, we sure do!

'If you don't paddle your own canoe, you don't move'
Katharine Hepburn

Task 1

'What are the reasons or conditions that are preventing you from reaching your goal?'

In other words, if it is something you really desire, what is stopping you from having it right now?

Before you can achieve any goal, you must know what stands in the way of its fulfilment. In answering this question make your list as comprehensive as possible. Note that it is important to include all the possible setbacks, blockading the road to realising your goals. This awareness helps prepare you to overcome all obstacles without any taking you by surprise.

If your goal was to run your own successful business, your answers to the above question could be something like this:
'I lack the education.'
'I fail to plan.'
'I don't have a clear idea of the business I would like to get into.'
'I have no capital.'
'I am afraid of the insecurity of not earning a fixed monthly salary.'

Remember a vital step to achieving your dreams is to find out what is preventing you from accomplishing them. If you know this, you are already halfway there.

Task 2

Now that you know each and every aspect stopping you from reaching your goal, next to each of these setbacks, write down the solutions needed to overcome every one of them.

You will find that these answers seem to flow effortlessly, simply and automatically. We have found from experience that there is a solution to almost any obstacle you may encounter.

Staying with the goal of running your own successful business, the solutions to the obstacles mentioned in **task 1** could be:

'I must study further in my chosen field.'

'I will become more organised by planning ahead.'

'I must research various business opportunities.'

'I must start saving and attempt to obtain a loan.'

'I will read about and speak to others who have succeeded in their own ventures to drive out insecurity.'

'I will keep my mind focused on the successful outcome of my goal.'

Task 3

So far you have listed the possible obstacles and the possible solutions to achieving your goal. Now you need to be more specific and write down in point form a step by step action plan on how you are going to achieve your goal.

If you were going to build a car from scratch, would you succeed without the necessary parts, tools and detailed assembly plan? Not likely! The same can be said for your plan of action. If it is not written down in the finest detail, you are highly unlikely to succeed.

The simplest way to list your action steps is to look at your end result (what you want to achieve) and work your way backwards one step at a time until you arrive at something you can do right now.

Staying again with the goal of running your own successful business, one of your final steps could entail looking at premises or interviewing new staff for your new business. You would work your steps back until you found something you can do today. This could be opening a savings or investment account, inquiring about relevant courses to attend or reading books on people who have successfully opened their own businesses.

By working your way backward from your ultimate goal, you can design the pathway to attaining your dreams.

Task 4

Once you have written down all the necessary action steps, assign a date of completion to each one of them.

In other words, we want you to decide upon a deadline for each action, writing it next to the relevant step. Why? Because once you commit yourself to a deadline, you are far more likely to act upon it, as having a set time frame becomes a challenge, which you cannot ignore. A deadline is to goal setting what a bow is to an arrow.

Task 5

Finally, after completing everything up to this stage, ask yourself this vital question: 'Is this goal of mine worthy enough for me to invest the time and effort necessary to achieve it?'

If your answer is 'yes', start today. If not, discontinue that goal.

If you have decided to follow through with your goal, on the top corner of your page, write down the date that you believe you will accomplish this goal.

As you complete each action step, tick it off. When all action steps are complete and you have achieved your goal, file this sheet in a special file marked 'goals accomplished.' On a miserable day when you are feeling down, there is nothing more motivating than going through this file and seeing the goals you have achieved.

You are now in the driver's seat!

Your written plans and deadlines will be your motivators, driving away procrastination and promoting both commitment and action. Writing out a step-by-step plan with dates for the completion of each action, somehow wills you not to let yourself down and urges you to stand up to the task you have set for yourself. You are now in the driver's seat;

you are in control. It is up to you to take action.

Most who have led successful lives are doers. They chose to take action and so can you!

Believe in yourself

If you think you are beaten, you are;
If you think you dare not; you don't;
If you'd like to win, but think you can't;
It's almost a cinch you won't.

If you think you'll lose, you're lost;
For out in the world we find
Success begins with a fellow's will,
It's all in the state of mind.
Life's battles don't always go
To the stronger or faster man;
But soon or late the man who wins
Is the one who thinks he can.

ANONYMOUS

Ever wondered why some people have it all; great jobs, loving relationships, financial success, health and happiness, while others seem doomed to constantly fail at everything they do?

There are also those who are not well educated, are disabled, come from a poor and difficult background or lack the necessary finances, yet they reach their dreams and make a success of themselves. While others who come from wealthy backgrounds, are well educated and have a clean bill of health, fail to excel, with success eluding them at every turn.

Are those that succeed more intelligent? Do they work harder? Do they work longer hours? Not likely! It all boils down to **BELIEF**. Those who succeed have an uplifting, confident and positive belief in themselves. They believe that they will succeed. Those who fail, have a poor image of themselves, believing before they've even begun that they will fail.

Belief is the expectation that what you want will actually happen. Our beliefs are like a compass that can help guide us towards our goals by promoting a feeling of certainty that we will get there. Merely hoping or wishing for something is useless. You must believe that it can and will be yours. If you believe strongly enough in yourself and your capabilities, you can do almost anything you set your mind to.

Beliefs hold incredible power, sometimes defying logic. There are numerous cases of 'mind over matter' whereby people achieved the 'impossible' only because they believed they could. Beliefs have even claimed the power to heal both mentally and physically, thereby baffling the medical profession.

To illustrate the power of belief, there have been studies involving people in hypnotic states actually burning their fingers because they were led to believe that the ice water they were dipping their fingers into was boiling water. Of course it was only ice water, but because they believed it to be boiling water, they sent this message to their brain and it reacted, resulting in burn marks and blisters. The brain simply does what it is told, acting upon what it believes to be true. The power and strength of one's will and belief cannot be underestimated. It is a massive force when handled correctly.

Where do our beliefs originate from?

By the tender age of 5, most of us have already had our full share of limiting beliefs drummed into us. We are bombarded with words like: 'Don't, you can't and no' from the moment we are born. During our schooling we are met with further limitations – 'You're not clever enough, you can't do it, you just haven't got it.' Is it any wonder that by the time we reach adulthood, without even realizing it, we have acquired a set of beliefs so limiting that we will never achieve even a fraction of our potential.

What beliefs have you inherited from your past? Were you made to believe that because your parents did not excel at school, you too would not? If your parents had to count every penny in order to survive, have you inherited the belief that money is hard to come by and that you are destined to live in poverty?

Remember that just one of these limiting beliefs can hold you back from creating the life you want. Choose your beliefs with care and get rid of those that limit you.

If you believe that you cannot succeed because there are no opportunities out there for you, you are absolutely correct. The only reason you see no opportunities is because you have conditioned yourself to believe just that. Indeed, you will never reap the benefits of all the opportunities out there, until you believe that these opportunities exist for you.

Whenever you doubt this, think of people who have yet to be born, who will eventually grab at the very opportunities you miss, rising to the top of their profession, running their own successful company and enjoying great wealth. Amongst them will also be those who are going to become the great leaders of tomorrow, Presidents of their Nation and athletic heroes. We believe you are one up on them as you are here now and they have yet to be born. So stop making excuses!

If you believe that you will fail, you will! If you believe that you will succeed, you will! If you believe you will be rich, you will be rich. If you believe you are destined for poverty, you will never rise above that. Those who achieve success in any form, value themselves highly. They choose to think rich thoughts and therefore receive the riches that life has to offer. **Remember that the bridge that leads to riches is built on rich thinking.**

How to develop belief in yourself

There is only one way to develop a powerful, positive and uplifting belief in yourself and that is to think only powerful, positive and uplifting thoughts. Think about it! If you have weak and negative thoughts all day long like, 'I'll never be successful. I'll never meet anyone nice. I always fail at what I do,' then you are doomed to fail, no matter what. So you better get used to it. To progress in life, your thoughts must be dominated by what you can do and not concentrated on what you cannot do. Remember *'Sooner or later the man that wins is the man that thinks he can.'*

Imagine an opportunity arose for you to go into your own business. What do you think your chances of success would be if your thoughts and beliefs were, 'I could be making a mistake. I may not make it on my own. I won't have any security. I always fail. The economy is bad'? Would you be confident, excited and motivated? Not likely, as you would be going into it half-heartedly, because your mind would be dominated by negative beliefs. Your chances of succeeding would be minimal.

However, what would your chances of succeeding be if your thoughts and beliefs were, 'I will make it work. I can do it. I will succeed no matter what'? Exceptionally good, as you have instructed your brain that you expect to succeed. You now act with excitement, motivation and confidence, tapping into your hidden potential. Just as failure feeds upon failure, success breeds success. The sky is now the limit!

We urge you to start now by believing that you are capable of the success you so deserve from life. Your beliefs hold great power. Exercise them now.

Believe you can and you will!

Don't fall into the mental trap of believing that 'you've either got it or you haven't and there is nothing you can do about it.' We can all 'have it,' if only we believe it's possible.

People have been known to achieve the 'impossible' when they were told they didn't stand a chance. They created miracles on the strength of their beliefs and accumulated enormous amounts of wealth and happiness when the odds of success were minimal, all because they had confidence and belief in their own ability.

Many would have thought that Helen Keller, who was left deaf, dumb and blind at the age of six, didn't stand a chance and that her odds of achieving success in any area of her life were minimal. Yet, by her belief in herself and her capabilities she went on to become an avid writer by the age of twenty. In 1904 she won an honours degree. She devoted her life to helping others like her, by writing numerous books, articles and giving lectures. Here was a woman who truly believed in herself and made it her life's work to help others believe in themselves.

If you believe 'I can,' you are correct. If you believe, 'I can't,' you are also completely correct. It is a fact that you become like the person you think and believe you are.

Utilise the Techniques of Affirmations and Visualisation

Imagine, see, feel and live your dreams as though you are there.
Tell yourself you have them
And soon they will be yours.
Warren Veenman & Sally Eichhorst

By now, you should have a clear idea of your goals, a burning desire to achieve them, a definite plan for their achievement, and belief in your capability to accomplish them. You are now ready to further explore and utilise some of the hidden powers you possess. Powers that are probably lying dormant in your mind but when utilised fully, will catapult you towards the achievement of your goals.

How do we tap into this vast ocean of power? Through utilising the techniques of affirmations and visualisation!

Affirmations

What is an affirmation? An affirmation is a simple, positive statement that you repeat to yourself over and over again. It illustrates what you would like to be and/or what you would like to acquire.

You can repeat them out loud or to yourself, whenever and wherever it suits you. This could be on your way to work, before you get up in the morning, waiting in a long queue, while you're jogging or before you go to bed at night.

Repetition Works!

There will be those of you who just cannot believe that anything you say repeatedly can have any effect on you. You could not be more mistaken!

Envisage each of your thoughts as a single droplet of rain and your mind as a dry piece of land. A single droplet of rain is quickly evaporated, just as a single thought is absorbed but rapidly forgotten. However, if the same droplet of rain is followed by a downpour of similar droplets, the dry land will be transformed into a powerful dam of life giving water, providing a well spring of energy and potential force. Likewise, the more your thoughts are repeated, the more powerful they become and the more able they are to transform themselves into reality.

By repeating thoughts or statements, day in and day out, you cross the line into the subconscious, resulting in it accepting these statements as true, making them beliefs and therefore becoming more determined to find ways to make them real.

Weak thoughts create weak forces
Strong thoughts create strong forces

Although what you are stating is not yet true or has not yet happened, you tend to live up to what you expect of yourself and begin to behave like the person you want to be. You automatically act and look for the opportunities to obtain what you want to have.

One thought at a time

As complex as the mind is, it can only hold one thought at any given time and this is why affirmations are so powerful. They fill your mind with those positive thoughts you continuously repeat, leaving no space for negative and destructive thoughts.

If you don't believe that your mind can only hold one thought at any given time, then try this little exercise. Close your eyes and think of a large waterfall crashing down a mountainside. Now at the same time, try to think of what you are going to do this evening. Impossible, isn't it? What you will find is that your mind will either think of the waterfall or what you are going to do tonight, not both at the same time. Your mind can change subjects very quickly, but it certainly cannot think of two things at the same time.

Tell your mind what you want it to believe

Whether you believe or disbelieve what you are saying to yourself makes no difference. Your brain cannot tell the difference between a statement that is real and one that is fabricated by you. In other words you are telling your mind what you want it to believe.

Many of you doubt the strength of affirmations to influence what you think or do, yet most of you have actually been practising the use of affirmations throughout your lives. However, these have been mostly negative affirmations.

How many of you have repeatedly said to yourselves:
'I can't do it'.
'I am stupid'.
'I am a failure'.
'I can't win'.
'I am not good enough'.

'I never have any opportunities in life'.

Looking at the last phrase, 'I never have any opportunities in life' – when you repeat this to yourself over and over again, what do you think your response will be when opportunity does knock on your door? Chances are, you won't hear it! You have convinced your mind to believe that there are no opportunities out there for you. You wouldn't notice an opportunity if it bit you on the leg or smacked you in the face!

On the other hand, if you continuously affirm to yourself, 'I have an abundance of opportunities', what will your response be now, when opportunity knocks on your door? Chances are, you will fling that door open on the first knock and welcome all opportunities with open arms! Why? Because you expect and believe that they are out there for you and you will actively look for them at every turn.

In this way affirmations are being successfully utilised by people from all corners of the globe and for countless reasons – business, sports, healing and socialising.

Guidelines to Formulating your Affirmations

Action Step1
Decide what you would like to affirm – it could be the desired outcome of your goal or a bad habit that you want to change. Remember that you can have as many affirmations as you like. A word of caution, as mentioned earlier, but worth repeating, is that you need not initially believe your statements. Don't try to force yourself to believe them as it is of little importance at this stage. For example, if you were repeating the affirmation made famous by the former Notre Dame Coach , Frank Leahy, *'When the going gets tough, the tough get going,'* and at the time you didn't really believe it, it is irrelevant, as through repetition you will eventually feel tough and ready to take on the world.

Action Step 2
Your affirmations must be in the present tense – in other words, 'I

will be friendly' is not an affirmation as 'will be' represents some future date that may never occur. Thus your mind won't be convinced of this statement and repeating it will have no effect. The solution would be to state what you want in the present tense by repeating, 'I am friendly.'

Action Step 3

Keep it positive – if your affirmation is, 'I am not uncomfortable with approaching strangers for new business,' at a glance it seems fine. But in reality, our mind does not recognise the word 'not' and instead takes in only 'uncomfortable.' Therefore it focuses only on 'uncomfortable with approaching strangers for new business,' thereby defeating the whole object of the exercise. The solution is to state what you want in the positive by repeating: 'I am comfortable with approaching strangers for new business.'

Action Step 4

Your affirmations can be written on separate cards, in your diary or in your personal journal. Keep it short and sweet. Obviously it is more difficult for the mind to absorb a long and involved statement than one that is short, precise and to the point. We keep our affirmations to less than eight words. Sometimes even two word affirmations can have a tremendous impact: ' I'm terrific' or 'I'm successful.'

Action Step 5

Read your affirmations no less than twice a day, every day. It is recommended that you read them first thing in the morning and just before you go to bed. In fact, read them and repeat them to yourself whenever and wherever the opportunity arises.

Don't expect results overnight

Have patience and things will happen in their own time. As long as you keep repeating your affirmations on a regular basis, they will eventually materialise into actions, resulting in the outcome you desire.

The Powerful Influence of Affirmations

A close friend of ours shared with us his story about the powerful influence affirmations had on his life.

'One of my very first goals was to run my own successful business. Affirmations worked wonders for me in realising this goal. I wrote my goal down on a card in the form of an affirmation and stuck it on my bathroom mirror. It read, 'I am running my own successful business.'

He continued, 'Every morning while I was shaving, the first thing I would see was my affirmation and because it was there and I had nothing better to look at, I would read this card over and over until I had finished in the bathroom.

'Although I was still working for somebody else and was in reality not running my own business, I found that by repeating this affirmation, I was a lot more driven and automatically focused on any opportunity that came my way to start my own business.

'When I eventually ran my first successful company, I framed this card to remind me of the power of written affirmations.'

Visualisation

The creative process known as visualisation makes use of your imagination to picture yourself already in possession of what you desire. This means picturing yourself doing what you would like to do, having what you would like to have or behaving like the person you want to be.

It is a fact that repetitively visualising what you want, will naturally result in your brain, like a 'Genie', getting to work at once trying to find ways of accomplishing your desire. You tap into the vast network of your brain, which automatically works on finding methods to accomplish your purpose.

When you paint a clear and brightly visual picture of what you want, you better equip your brain to make it happen for you. If you really picture something, seeing it as clear as day in your mind and bringing back the image again and again, your brain will eventually begin to believe it is really there. This belief results in all your actions being geared towards the attainment of your goal, in turn transforming the visualisation into reality.

Again, as with affirmations, it does not matter whether you believe your visualisation or not. Remember that the mind cannot distinguish between what is real and what is imagined. So use this powerful tool to your benefit, by 'fooling' your mind into guiding you towards your goal.

Don't confuse visualisation with the simple act of daydreaming. Unlike daydreams, visualisation is a powerful tool, creating enough force and energy to stoke the fires of your burning desire.

How to Visualise Productively

1. **Before you can visualise productively, decide upon a clear and precise idea of what you want to have or be**.
   Perhaps you want to meet someone special, become a better speaker, run your own business, achieve enormous wealth or live in that dream house by the seaside.

2. **Find a nice peaceful place**.
   It may be in the house, garden or park, as long as there are none of the disturbances, distractions or noises that usually raise the blood pressure and stress levels. It could even be lying in bed before you start your day, sitting in your office during lunch or in the evening on the couch with the lights dimmed.

3. **Now relax, close your eyes and feel all the muscles in your body slowly unwinding**.

   Remain in this position for about 5 minutes. Let your thoughts wander freely. At this stage do not force yourself to think about anything. This will clear the mind of all roadblocks, opening your imagination to all ideas and possibilities, making visualisation a lot more effective.

4. **Now slowly focus your thoughts on what you decided upon in step 1**.

   It is important that you visualise it as though it has already happened. In other words, see yourself living in the house you want, driving the car you desire or speaking effectively in front of a large audience. It is imperative that you visualise your goal right down to the finest detail. Think of all the things associated with the goal and use them to draw a mental picture of the desired outcome.

   For example, let's say that your goal is to own a new car. In your mind you need to see the model of the car, see the make of the car, see the colour of the car and see its interior. You must mentally picture the car from outside to inside, top to bottom, right down to the finest detail. You should also see yourself in the driver's seat, driving the car home, seeing the car parked in your garage and watching your family and friends admiring the car. In this way, you are visualising the reality you desire. You are living in your mind as if you already have the car.

   By regularly picturing and living your desired outcome in your imagination, it becomes increasingly real and you will want it all the more. It feeds your desire, driving you to take action to make it happen for yourself.

5. **The final step in visualisation is to utilise as many of your senses as possible**.

   How are you feeling when you are giving a perfect speech in front of thousands of people? Feel that feeling of excitement and ecstasy when they give you a standing ovation at the end. When visualising your dream car, smell its leather interior and touch its smooth metallic surface.

Go so far as to imagine the feeling of pride that goes with owning your dream car. Imagine the feeling of sitting behind the wheel with the sunroof down, the wind in your hair as you travel down the highway. Would you feel ecstatically happy, deliciously content, gloriously excited or unbelievably proud?

Whatever you feel, really live and experience it as though you already have it. Walk tall with pride and shiver in excited anticipation at the picture of sitting at the wheel of your very own dream car. Really see, feel and ultimately experience the joy of achieving your goal.

Obtaining the Full Benefits of Visualisation

As with affirmations, your visualisations must be repeated over and over to have any effect. It is no use trying once or twice, then sitting back waiting for everything to fall into your lap. As with anything worthwhile, it takes time and effort. You must continue with this exercise at least twice a day, every day, three hundred and sixty five days a year. We recommend that you create your mental picture first thing in the morning and last thing in the evening. Do this every single day until you eventually achieve your goal. Remember that there is immense power in repetition and it is this repetition and consistency, which gives visualisation its strength, distinguishing it from idle daydreaming. So the importance of repetition cannot be over stressed.

Initially you may find it difficult to focus on your specific goal, as your lazy mind is not used to concentrating for so long on a specific idea. This is quite normal! When your mind does wander, gently bring it back, focusing again on your specific goal. You will find that practice makes perfect and you will soon be able to control your mind and direct it as you wish.

It is crucial that you always visualise your goal in the present, as though it is happening right now. You must also visualise the steps leading up to the desired outcome. For example, if you are visualising owning a new car, you would see yourself contacting the car dealer, making an appointment and taking the car for a test drive.

Make sure that the image you are visualising is seen through your own eyes and not through the eyes of an onlooker. For example, if you were giving a presentation to prospective clients, you would not be on the sideline watching yourself talk. Instead you would be facing the members head on while you conducted the presentation.

The power to influence your thoughts

You alone have the power to choose what you think about all day long. You have total control of this one thing, your thoughts. It is through the power of affirmations and visualisation that you are able to influence your thoughts. Together, affirmations and visualisation develop within you an extremely powerful and inspiring belief in yourself and your ability to reach your goal.

Now that you know what you want, have a burning desire to achieve it, devised a plan for its achievement and developed belief in its attainment, you are well on the road to accomplishing your goal. When you apply affirmations to your goal plus regularly visualising yourself already in possession of your goal, you can already see the finishing line. However, you still need one vital ingredient to get you there............ ...

Chapter 20

Step 6 — How to attain your dreams

Perseverance

'Great works are performed not by strength, but by perseverance.'
Samuel Johnson, 'Rasselas'

Think back to the day when you first climbed behind the wheel of a car to learn to drive. Remember the first time you sat nervously in the driver's seat and clutched the steering wheel in your hands. There was so much to think about all at once – coordinating the clutch with the gears whilst using the correct footing for the brakes, accelerator and clutch. At the same time concentrating on the indicators, focusing on all the mirrors, never mind the endless road signs and nerve-wracking traffic. Eventually it all fell into place and you had unknowingly learnt to drive by following the principles we outlined in goal setting.

Firstly, you knew without the slightest doubt that you wanted to learn to drive. This was your goal!

Secondly, you created a burning desire by analyzing the personal rewards and benefits you stood to gain from learning to drive. Your friends may have been driving already and you were tired of relying on them or your parents for transport.

Thirdly, you planned it. You set aside the dates and times when friends and family could help you. You made appointments with the local driving school. When you were ready, you booked your driving test.

Fourthly, you developed belief in yourself. Belief that you would eventually accomplish this goal. Of course you had seen thousands of people driving cars, but now it was different because it was you. You had to convince yourself that you too could do it.

Next, you probably lay awake at night or early in the morning visualizing yourself driving comfortably in peak hour traffic. You must have repeatedly affirmed to yourself that 'I can do this' or 'I can drive'!

There remains one final step that you must have done if you eventually achieved your goal. If you successfully completed all the above steps but still never learnt to drive a car, it is obvious that you lacked this vital ingredient. Sadly, most people seem to accomplish all the steps above when aiming for their ultimate goals in life, but because they lack this one important ingredient, they fail.

Whilst learning to drive, with sweaty palms and numerous nightmarish stalls, when nothing seemed to go your way, did you give up? Or, when those irate drivers blew their hooters at you for stalling in front of them, cutting them off or driving too slowly, did you persist until you achieved your drivers' license? If you did, you **persevered**, thereby making use of the final and vital quality necessary to succeed in anything.

Don't wave the flag of defeat!

Perseverance should not be confused with 'hard work' or 'the number of hours worked'. It can be more accurately defined as your total commitment and determination to follow through with your plan, even in the face of defeat and criticism. It is knowing what you want and being so determined to have it that you commit your entire efforts to getting it. It means having the willpower to fight on when others wave the flag of defeat. It is the quality that truly separates the winners from the losers.

To succeed in anything, you must learn to develop perseverance, or else you will fail, no matter how worthy your goal.

Is it worth it?

The question is, how do you develop perseverance? Quite simply, what you are striving for must be worth it to you! To explain this, take yourself back to the Chapter in which we discussed desire in detail. Remember that if you have enough reasons to do something, you will be far more motivated to do it. It must be worth the time, effort and resources you must sacrifice to achieve it.

The more intense your desire, the more determined you will be to persist until you have accomplished your goal. Combine this intense desire with strong willpower and self-confidence and your recipe for perseverance is complete. Your desire will feed you with the energy needed to pick yourself up and start again, whilst your self-confidence and will-power will shield you from the effects of criticism, urging you to go on, ignoring the pessimism and negativity around you. Together all these things will encourage you to persevere and eventually succeed.

This solid, unyielding perseverance will guide you through your plan, picking you up when you fall and bulldozing through roadblocks that stand in your way to reaching your goal.

The secret is to try again

Unfortunately, research has found that the majority of people lack perseverance, choosing rather to turn and run for the hills when faced with their first setback. It is only a handful of people that push on along the rocky road to reaching their dreams.

Perseverance makes all the difference between failing and winning! Without perseverance you have lost before you have even begun. No matter how often you fall and are knocked back down again and again; the spirit of the true champion is found in those who pick themselves up every time to try again.

When you have perseverance you will win even when the deck is stacked against you. 'If at first you don't succeed, try and try again' – this old and well used phrase is the essence of perseverance.

To truly enjoy the pot of gold at the end of the rainbow, you must be prepared to face a long and sometimes treacherous journey. Nothing for nothing! It is a fact that without perseverance you are destined to achieve nothing.

> *'A quitter never wins and a winner never quits'*
> **Napoleon Hill.**

You can develop perseverance!

You can develop perseverance with a little effort. As with happiness, sadness and aggression, perseverance is a state of mind, which you can alter and train. Anyone, regardless of their background and intellectual capacity, can develop perseverance by following the few easy guidelines below.

1. You must work on developing a strong willpower.

2. Learn from your failures and use what you have learnt to your advantage on your next attempt.

3. You must make some progress every day towards the attainment of your goal – no matter how small.

4. Realise that a lack of perseverance is a bad habit, which can be eradicated by practising again and again the art of perseverance. For example, finish the painting you started, finish the study course you started ages ago, finish building the fish pond you never seem to find the time to complete. Practise perseverance with things in your every day life and it will soon become a habit.

Stop making excuses and start finding solutions

Whilst travelling towards your goal, you will encounter many stumbling blocks. This is when you must call upon the quality of perseverance so you may succeed where others have failed. Don't follow those who turn back at the slightest sign of trouble. Rather, join those who reach their goals, by overcoming all obstacles along the way and never giving up on their dreams.

We tend to give up too soon, blaming everything but ourselves:
'I never had the opportunities to study further.'
'I came from a poor upbringing and it has held me back.'
'It's the economy that keeps me down.'

It's time you stop making excuses and start finding solutions.

Concentrate on the big picture

It is important that you concentrate on the big picture, which is the achievement of your goal and not on short-term fixes. This can be seen in people who want to lose weight but never quite seem to get there. They have a planned diet to follow, but get tempted by the short-term fix of 'feel good food' like sweets and junk food. This makes them feel great for a short period of time, but results in them losing sight of their long-term goal of weight loss. Likewise with all types of goals, people tend to sacrifice their long-term goals for short-term fixes. Those who succeed are those who are able to sacrifice short term fixes for the attainment of their ultimate goal, giving them 100% satisfaction. You must decide if you would rather have 2% of your goal now or 100% at your target date. Winners aim for 100%.

Without perseverance you will not win and the rewards you dreamed of will always remain out of your grasp; a mere figment of your imagination. Perseverance is probably the single most important quality anyone who is interested in succeeding could ever possess. Develop this quality and it will carry you when you are down, lifting you and urging you to push on until you reach your dreams.

Chapter 21

Dreams can come true

DREAM A LITTLE DREAM......

My wish became a dream.
My dream matured into a solid and strong goal.
My goal grew further, sparking off my desire until it became a raging fire,
urging me to act.
My burning desire chased me, pushed me and inspired me to get moving.
It would not allow me even a seconds rest, forcing me to devise a plan of
action to escape its flames.
But I was not alone.
Belief was there, taking my hand, supporting me wholeheartedly and leading
me to safety.
Belief allowed me to see that I could have anything I truly wanted.
Belief introduced me to the inner-power of my mind and together we all
envisaged and lived my dream, bringing it closer than ever before to realities
door.
Here I met perseverance, who took hold of my other hand, sometimes pulling
me, pushing me and often carrying me as I stumbled again and again.
Perseverance would not let me quit and together we reached the goal post.
Now I am living my dream; my ultimate life.
I have learnt that the only failure in life is to never dream and to never try
hard enough to reach your dreams.

Sally Eichhorst

You now have the 'tools' to accomplish all that you desire. We recommend that you start out by writing a minimum of 2 goals, which should be achievable within a seven-day period. Doing this on a regular, weekly basis will ensure that goal setting and achieving your goals become second nature to you. Before you know it, you will be an experienced goal setter, setting more ambitious goals and pleasantly surprising yourself by achieving them well within your time frame.

As we have mentioned earlier, just casually reading through this book and not partaking in the exercises will be of little benefit to you. However, by following the steps we have outlined in the previous Chapters on goal setting, you will unquestionably reach your ultimate dreams.

Take some time out to complete all the exercises – it will not be time wasted! Successful goal setting will help you to design the life you have always dreamed of. How can it not be worth your while?

Does this work? You bet it does! We have successfully practised goal setting for the past decade and have so far both achieved all that we set out to do. We have since set new goals and are striving for their achievement at this very moment. We are both living the lives we want right now and we still have so much more to look forward to.

It has worked for us as well as numerous others. It is now up to you to make it work for yourself by applying it to your life. We can only show you how; the rest is up to you!

Part 5

Use Your Mind and Body to Overcome All

The mind and body are essentially one
As a team, they can work wonders,
Overcoming any problem and managing any situation.
Warren Veenman & Sally Eichhorst

Chapter 22

Got a problem?

Life is a series of tests!
We fall upon these stumbling blocks
Scared, confused and unaware of what lies ahead
We meet our selfish problems
Some crumble at the thought of facing their Goliath,
While others seize the challenge and chip their mountains down.
Life's battle once more victorious as our mountain crumbles,
Only to be replaced by another.
Why conquer at all when the battle seems an endless one?
Why not throw in the towel?
Crawl into an untainted world where we crumble into oblivion before our mountains.
No!
Are we not naturally curious?
Do we not want to see what lies beyond our mountain?
It is the hope of finding a Garden of Eden on the other side!
It is in the conquering that we grow and become larger than the mountains which
plague us.
Hope is the key;
And the driving spirit that makes us conquerors, the locksmith.
Together they build upon one another,
And soon outweigh the largest of all Goliaths.
Such is life!

Sally Eichhorst

Got a problem? Great! Why? Because it means it is time for you to grow again!

Whenever you repeatedly conquer your problems, you grow as a person, becoming stronger, wiser and more knowledgeable. You also become more experienced to cope with the future problems that life hands you.

> *'Continually triumphing over your problems*
> *will be the stepping stones to your success in life.'*
> **Warren Veenman & Sally Eichhorst**

Find the above words hard to believe? Then cast your mind back:

Firstly, think back to any accomplishment in your life. Probably, you'll discover that your accomplishment was due to a problem you had to face and overcome. In fact, if you look at any person who has achieved anything in their lives, you will notice that their success was also due to problems they had to face and conquer.

Secondly, think back to an obvious mistake you've recently made. Before you start kicking yourself all over again, stop and take a closer look at the overall outcome. You will probably discover that you have learnt and grown more from that one experience than you have from anything else that week, month or even year.

> *'A life spent in making mistakes is not only more honourable*
> *but more useful than a life spent doing nothing.'*
> **George Bernard Shaw, 'The Doctor's Dilemma', preface**

When you are willing to see your problems in this new light, you will recognise the opportunities they hide and meet the challenges they present. The reason why so many people fail to recognise opportunity, is that they think opportunity will someday come knocking on their door and say, 'Hi, I'm opportunity!' Well, we've got news for them! Opportunity does not usually show itself. It doesn't come down from the sky like a bolt of lightening. It usually comes disguised. Yes! Opportunities usually have a sneaky way of masking themselves as problems, misfortunes and failures.

> *'The only one that makes no mistakes is one who never does anything!'*
> **Theodore Roosevelt, saying inscribed on the Theodore Roosevelt Birthplace National**
> **Historic Site, New York City**

Solving 99% of your problems

Below is a 6-step plan we have devised, to help you solve 99% of your problems.

One: **Write down precisely what the problem is.**
Get a sheet of blank paper and write down a detailed description of what the problem is. You will find that writing your problem down, has the magical quality of making you think far more accurately and clearly about your problem.
For example: My car is old and keeps breaking down.

Two: **Write down the solution you want to achieve**
Now write down underneath your problem what you would like the outcome to be. If need be, close your eyes and spend a few minutes thinking about it. At this stage don't worry about how to achieve it, just concentrate on the outcome you want. If you have a clear idea of what you want, then you can devise an effective plan to get there. If you are not sure of what you want the outcome to be, then how can you even begin to construct a plan of action and weigh up various solutions?
For example: I want to own a better car that is reliable and won't keep breaking down.

Three: **Write down a minimum of 3 possible solutions to your problem.**
Be careful not to fall into the trap of making a decision on the first, most obvious or easiest solution that pops into your head. We all have at some stage or another made hasty decisions to solve our problems and later looked back and regretted making the wrong decision. Remember that there are many roads to the same destination. So take the time now to list as many solutions as you can think of.
For example: 1. I will purchase a brand new car.
                2. I will fix my old car with the little savings I've got.
                3. I will trade my car in for a good second hand car.

Four: **Next to each solution, write down the possible results.**

For example, next to each of the above solutions I could write:

1. It would be great to have a brand new car, but I would have to pay it off over the next 4 years. This is a big responsibility and I would have to sacrifice a lot of other things.
2. If I fix my old car, there is still a strong chance that it will break down again. I foresee myself spending all my savings on repairing my car with the risk of it still breaking down.
3. I could get a reasonable amount for my car as a trade in and I'm pretty sure I could purchase a good second hand car at a price I can afford.

Five: **Make a decision on one of your solutions**

Once you have scrutinised each of the solutions, make a decision on the solution that best solves your problem and don't look back. Don't procrastinate! Remember that pondering about a problem for too long, beyond a certain point can actually be destructive as worry and fear creep in.

For example: I will trade my car in for a good second hand one.

Six: **Set a deadline for its completion**

The value of setting a target date cannot be over emphasised. Once you commit yourself to a target date, you are far more likely to act upon it. Having a set time frame becomes a challenge, which you cannot ignore. So don't ignore your problem.

Still cannot solve that problem?

Sometimes, try as you may, you simply cannot find a solution to your problem. Now what?

This is where your subconscious mind, that brilliant, yet hidden and often under-utilised part of you can come to the rescue. By following the 3 steps below, you can make use of your subconscious mind to help you solve the most pressing of problems.

This exercise should take a mere five minutes. We recommend that it be done before you fall asleep at night, as this is when you are usually at your most relaxed. The idea is to fall asleep with the knowledge that your problem is now in the hands of your subconscious. You can rest easy with the thought that your subconscious (which never rests or sleeps) will get to work to provide you with your solution(s).

One:

> Close your eyes and relax. Feel all the muscles in your body slowly unwinding. You should feel as if you are floating on water, with no stress on your muscles, joints and mind. Just let your thoughts come and go as they please. Don't force yourself to think of anything. Just relax. Once you are feeling sufficiently relaxed and comfortable you are ready for step 2.

Two:

> Now think of the problem that you want solved. Tell your subconscious exactly what the problem is and ask it to reveal the solution(s) to you. Keep repeating this over and over to yourself, as it is through repetition that your message will eventually reach the depths of your subconscious mind. Don't try to think of the answer. Just let your subconscious be aware that you want a solution to this problem. Remember that your subconscious has an abundance of information and the solutions to all your problems are there. This wellspring of knowledge is just waiting for you to tap into it.

Three:

> Don't let the problem worry you anymore. It is now in the capable hands of your subconscious. Just drop off to sleep with the confident belief that the answers will soon be revealed to you.

Whenever we do this exercise we are amazed at how quickly the solutions come to us. Sometimes, it's first thing as we open our eyes in the morning. Other times it could be while we are getting ready for work, drinking our morning coffee, driving in the car or standing in a jam-packed elevator. In fact, the answer(s) pop into our minds just about anywhere.

Call it a hunch. Call it insight. Call it instinct. Call it whatever you want, but what it really is, is a message from your subconscious.

Using lateral thinking to solve problems

When looking for a solution to any problem, it is vital to open your mind to all possibilities. Often we are too narrow-minded to see an obvious solution and later regret overlooking the obvious.

Many of us miss out on all sorts of opportunities or give up too soon, all because we are not thinking laterally and allowing for every possibility.

Are you a lateral thinker?

The following riddle will test your lateral thinking ability. The answer is on the last page of this book.

A policeman is walking past a brick wall when he hears the following plea, 'No John, don't shoot me!' A shot is fired from a gun! Now he can't see what is going on, as the wall is too high. So he runs around the wall to see what happened.

To his shock he sees a man lying dead on the ground. Next to the dead man is a gun and standing in front of the dead man are the three suspects. One is a butcher, one is a builder and one is a lawyer.

Now, the policeman has never seen any of these people before, so he does not know any of their names. Furthermore, he does not even know what their professions are. He doesn't speak to them and before they can utter one word, he walks over to the lawyer and arrests him!

How did he know it was the lawyer?

Face up to the challenge

We all have problems. It's a fact of life! What is important however is our attitude towards these problems and how we deal with them.

From now on, try to see problems from a new perspective. Don't be afraid of them. In fact, instead of running away from them, actively seek them out and confront them.

You should always be on the look out for new problems, or rather 'new challenges' to keep your thinking processes well oiled and practised. Learn to become comfortable with change, confident in facing up to the unknown and at ease with facing up to the 'challenges' of life.

It is from the conquering of your problems that you grow in life
and attain the success you desire.
Warren Veenman & Sally Eichhorst

Chapter 23

The powerful influence of Physiology

'The body says what words cannot.'
Martha Graham, interview, 'The New York Times' March 31, 1985

In this chapter it is our aim to convey to you the powerful influence your physiology has on your mental state. The way you walk, talk, breathe, your facial expressions, your every move, even the tension of your muscles has a tremendous influence on your brain.

It works the other way as well! Your state of mind has a tremendous influence on your physiology as they are both inter-linked. If you had to change the one it would most definitely affect the other.

Body language = mental state

Think back to a day when you felt completely rundown. Perhaps you were tired, depressed, suffering from a hang over or on the verge of an unwelcome dose of the flu. Whatever the case, you certainly felt miserable and you probably emphasised this by slouching your shoulders and breathing heavily with a deep frown on your face.

Now think back to a day when you felt on top of the world. Your body portrayed a completely different picture. Now your shoulders were back as you stood straight and tall. Your chin was up and you probably had a great big grin stretching from ear to ear. No doubt you would find that your breathing was deep, even and leisurely. You even moved with energetic determination and confidence.

Notice how the two are linked? When your state of mind is negative and disgruntled, your body paints the same picture. Likewise, when your state of mind is positive and happy, your body paints a similar picture of happiness. This is also true in the reverse as the picture your body paints through your posture, breathing, movements, expressions etc, can change your state of mind.

Are we saying that if you push your chest out, pull your shoulders back, stand straight and tall and put a big grin on your face, that this can change the way you are feeling? You bet!

Try this!

Don't believe us? Then why don't you try this quick exercise? Jump up, put a big smile on your face, throw your shoulders back, stand up straight and proud, lift your head up high, take a few steps walking briskly with a sense of purpose and direction. Even whistle your favourite tune.

Now how do you feel? You will find that you'll feel great, even if you were feeling depressed a few moments ago. What happened? By creating this positive physiology, the same mental state will naturally follow, as your brain is receiving a message from your body to be energetic and dynamic. In answer, it will do just that and you will feel wonderful.

Remember that it works in the reverse as well. If you were to look down, drop your head, slump your shoulders and walk around dragging your feet, you would no doubt find that this negative physiology you have created would result in a negative mental state, causing you to feel all gloomy and flat.

So we can see what a brilliantly powerful tool physiology is when trying to alter our mental state.

Make your physiology work for you

You can use this tool to enable you to handle any situation, even those you once feared or felt incapable of managing. Next time you need to approach someone, attend an interview, give an important speech or canvass for new business, change your physiology to suit the situation.

If you are afraid of approaching someone, change your physiology by appearing to be confident. Simply use your body to help you 'pretend' to be confident and sure of yourself. Walk towards that person with head held high, breathing easily with a broad, open smile on your face. In this way you will fool your mind into thinking you can do this and you feel happy and confident about it. The end result is that you will actually become confident and feel you can do it. Now you see what a marvellous tool this is!

A word of advice when utilising this tool, is that any changes you make in your physiology must be strong, definite and obvious enough for the brain to interpret clearly, otherwise it won't know exactly how to react.

If you say to yourself, 'I may as well try this although I wonder whether it will have any affect on my mood' and then you half-heartedly attempt to make changes to your physiology. What happens? Your brain is confused as you are sending it feeble and conflicting messages. You certainly won't attain the state you desire in this way. The changes you make in your physiology must be absolutely clear and definite to attain the desired result.

Attracting the things you want with physiology

We want you to try this positive and uplifting exercise.

Firstly, think of something you would really like to have more of. It could be friends, wealth, happiness, confidence, knowledge or good humour.

From this moment on, allow others to believe that you already possess plenty of what it is you want. How? By using your physiology to pretend you already have it. By doing this, you will in turn convince your mind that you indeed have it. As we discussed earlier in this book, once you have convinced your mind of something, it will be determined to find ways to make it real. 'What the mind dwells upon, it believes. What it believes, it attracts.'

If you convince your mind through your physiology that you are confident, you will indeed become confident and behave accordingly. If you convince your mind that you are wealthy, it will attract wealth to you. Beware that the opposite is also true – poverty breeds poverty and fearful thoughts create fearful experiences. So rather create an aura around you that spells 'happiness and prosperity'.

We assure you that this works! Try it! Remember that you cannot possibly remain down in the dumps when your body is portraying an ecstatically happy picture to your mind. Your mind will soon be convinced to follow suit. It works!

In Conclusion

'Unleash the power you have within you and live your life to the full!
Warren Veenman & Sally Eichhorst

To conclude our journey with you, we would like to remind you of a few vital points covered in our book.

♦ Never forget that the happiness so sought after in life has nothing to do with who we are, what we have, where we are or where we are going. It has everything to do with the thoughts we feed our mind. Happiness in life is but a state of mind and with the right positive thoughts, we can acquire that state of mind.

♦ Remember that you are what you think! If you radically change your thoughts for the better, you will radically change your life for the better. In other words, the situations and material conditions you attract in life are a result of the thoughts you dwell upon. So choose to think only positive thoughts and to promote a positive state of mind. Choose also to banish negative thoughts and states of fear, depression and worry, which can only limit your life.

♦ We have witnessed the tremendous healing power of having the right thoughts. We have seen its ability to entirely change so many lives. *'No matter what your present situation; whether you are on the verge of a nervous break down through worry and anxiety, riddled with stress and tension, facing a colossal problem, morbidly depressed, or paralyzed with fear, you can avoid and banish all these situations forever, with the right thoughts and the resultant positive mental attitude.'*

♦ We believe beyond a shadow of a doubt in the power of thoughts to transform and enrich all lives. It has been proved time and time again and it has worked for us.

♦ You must believe that there are no limits to your potential other than those you have set for yourself. So believe in yourself and you will astound yourself with your capabilities.

♦ If you believe 'I can,' you are correct. If you believe, 'I can't,' you are also completely correct. It is a fact that you become like the person you think and believe you are.

♦ We urge you now and always to try and rediscover the child within you. That child which knows no fear, no worries, no limitations and has a healthy appetite for life and the challenges it has to offer.

♦ You must realise that there is only one way to make the best of the future and that is to put the past behind you and make the best of today. Don't wait for an age, a stage in your life or a dream to come true to really live – live now and enjoy this moment, this hour and every day of your life.

♦ 'Today' will never dawn again. 'Today' is a precious gift that can slip away with alarming speed. Wasted, it will eat a chunk out of your life, but lived well, it will fulfil your life and make it whole.

♦ If you haven't yet, start now and make the best of every precious day. Know what you want from life and follow our goal-setting program to achieve it. Successful goal setting will help you to design the life of which you have always dreamed. Remember that we can only show you how; the rest is up to you!

♦ Once more we repeat that just casually reading through this book and not partaking in the exercises will be of little benefit to you. If you have not yet completed all the exercises, take some time now to do so – it most certainly will not be time wasted!

♦ Most importantly, unleash your full potential and live your ultimate life!

A final exercise

Every time you sit back and re-evaluate your life (we recommend the 1st of every month) we want you to ask yourself the following 10 questions and answer them with complete honesty. When you can honestly answer 'yes' to every single question, you are not only on the right road to achieving your dreams; you are already there!

1. Do you have a clear and precise idea of what you want to achieve in life?

2. Do you have an intense, burning desire within you to achieve your goals and do you constantly stoke this fire to keep it alive?

3. Do you have a written plan to achieve your major goals in life, a date for their accomplishment and are you at this very moment actively pursuing your goals?

4. Have you developed a powerful, positive and uplifting belief in yourself and your capabilities, by only thinking powerful, positive and uplifting thoughts?

5. Are you making use of affirmations and visualisation to develop within you an extremely powerful and inspiring belief in yourself and your ability to reach your goals?

6. Do you persevere? Have you developed this quality so that it will carry you when you are down, lifting you and urging you to push

on until you reach your dreams?

7. Do you choose to think only positive thoughts and to promote a positive state of mind, choosing to banish negative thoughts and states of fear, depression and worry, which can only limit your life?

8. Do you live every day as though it were your last, making the best of every moment? This means not procrastinating, wasting time or living in the past.

9. Are you aware of the powerful influence your physiology has on your mental state and are you currently using this effectively potent tool to benefit you?

10. Are you happy with your life and where it's going? If not, have you made the necessary changes to ensure future happiness?

Wake up and Enjoy Life!
It's yours for the taking.
Your Life, your Time, your Move.
Make that Move! Get up and Make it Happen.
Only you can change your life.
Find the Will and the Means will soon follow.
Reach deep down inside and find out who you are and what you really want.
Dreams do come true, but don't wait around for good things to happen to you- Make them Happen!
It's never too late to change your Life and Make a Difference.
It's all up to you.
You can do it!

Sally Eichhorst

Answer to lateral thinking riddle
The butcher and the builder are both women. The only man was the lawyer. So he must have been John.

Any correspondence or enquiries regarding other books by
the same authors can be addressed to :
Reach Publishers
P.O.Box 1384
Wandsbeck
South Africa
3631